The Sacred Now

The Sacred Now

Cultivating Jewish Spiritual Consciousness

Mark Elber

WIPF & STOCK · Eugene, Oregon

THE SACRED NOW
Cultivating Jewish Spiritual Consciousness

Wipf & Stock
An Imprint of Wipf and Stock Publishers
199 W. 8th Ave., Suite 3
Eugene, OR 97401

www.wipfandstock.com

PAPERBACK ISBN: 978-1-5326-1759-1
HARDCOVER ISBN: 978-1-4982-4239-4
EBOOK ISBN: 978-1-4982-4238-7

Manufactured in the U.S.A.   JULY 14, 2017

This book is dedicated to my beloved family:
Shoshana, Lev, and Mira

Contents

Introduction

It was the week after Thanksgiving, 1967. I was not quite sixteen years old when one afternoon, while walking up 43rd Street towards Queens Boulevard in Sunnyside, Queens, the heft of the elevated subway looming on the horizon, in a moment my life changed forever. Suddenly, everything I looked at felt utterly alive, pulsing with Divinity. Everything seemed obviously and palpably part of God, part of the One, including myself, though I had lost any sense of a separate "self" for the duration of the experience. The entire experience was one long peak. For whatever reason, this state of consciousness became very common for me for the next four years or so. I could virtually enter it at will.

A philosophically inclined teenager, I had been studying Plato and Aristotle on my own and learning Talmud privately with a couple of Yeshiva students about ten years older than I, young men who attended the same synagogue in which I had grown up, an Orthodox *shul* called Young Israel of Sunnyside. In response to my initial ecstatic encounter I formulated for myself an understanding of God, creation, our role in it, and the function of Judaism and *mitzvot*. Though this sounds embarrassingly grandiose, it felt quite natural to me at the time.

I had never heard of experiences of this nature, however, and naively assumed that they must be what all Orthodox Jews experience regularly, since I had become quite "Orthodox" or

"Orthoprax" in the previous few months (a practice towards which I had been evolving from the point of my becoming a Bar Mitzvah). I mentioned the experience to a couple of my Orthodox friends. They seemed to have no idea what I was talking about. At first I was confused. I thought I had just discovered or happened upon something Orthodox Jews had always known! It seemed obvious to me that this overwhelming consciousness of God's all-pervasive Presence was the point and goal of all Jewish ritual practice. Gradually, I realized I should probably not speak about these experiences, because they seemed so foreign, perhaps even aberrant, to others.

It was the following autumn when I entered college that I became exposed to Kabbalah and Hasidism (via Chabad/Lubavitch initially) and discovered a traditional Jewish vocabulary and perspective that was essentially synonymous with what I had articulated to myself. I knew I had to delve more deeply into this part of the Jewish tradition.

For years I felt I should be "Orthodox," yet, despite my very Jewishly observant life, I always felt my ultimate allegiance was to God, rather than to "Orthodoxy." I also recognized the holiness inherent in secular life and saw the dichotomy people commonly made between "secular" and "spiritual" as fundamentally erroneous. But it wasn't until I became exposed to serious feminist thinking in the early 1970s that I stopped feeling at all apologetic for not being truly "Orthodox."

My parents were Polish Jews who arrived on America's shores in June 1949. They themselves had been raised in Orthodox households. My mother's immediate family was Zhidichoiv Hasidim, but she was the rebel in the family, a fact that saved her life while her parents and her four brothers perished during the Holocaust. While my parents' own practice of Polish Orthodox Judaism did not survive World War II, they retained the perspective that it was the most genuine expression of Judaism. I had imbibed my parents' bias that the vanished world of Polish Orthodoxy (which was mostly kept alive in our house in legend) was authentic Judaism, next to which everything else paled. Yet, even though I had absorbed this prejudice, I did not confuse religiosity or spirituality with observance. I could readily see that there were very Jewishly observant people who apparently were not particularly "spiritual" or "religious," and people who were not at all observant yet were very spiritually attuned and "religious." Because my parents were no longer all that observant themselves, I didn't confuse how "Jewish" a person was with how "observant" a person was, despite the fact that these were notions I regularly encountered. That also led me to distinguish between "Jewishness" and "Judaism."

This is the background and foreground of this book. For well over forty years the desire to present this material and to articulate its repercussions has been gestating within me. And yet, even now, I struggle to find the right words. I see the Jewish tradition as a treasure of great spiritual, moral, psychological, and intellectual insights that belongs to those of us who embrace it, engage it, and struggle with it. No one has a monopoly on it—no denomination, no rabbi, no thinker.

At best we may contribute to the discussion. At the same time, it's obvious that Judaism and Jewishness have evolved through time. Biblical Judaism is not identical with Rabbinic Judaism, despite what fundamentalists say to rationalize a belief that all "Torah" comes literally from Sinai. Symbolically or figuratively that's a beautiful way of connecting us to our sacred mythology, but taken literally it's fundamentally flawed. There's no need to make that case here. There are plenty of accessible books that present that argument persuasively if the reader doesn't have the preconception that the Torah, both written and oral, is the literal word of the Eternal One.

I recognize that we often continue an argument with our past even if the people we're attempting to refute stopped arguing long ago. Because my formative Jewish spiritual awakening occurred in an Orthodox and Hasidic setting, I may still be justifying all my reasons for ultimately leaving it and excessively addressing those old voices. Yet in my heart and mind (as far as I am aware), I have no desire to convince anyone of any particular dogmas, but rather to present and explore a Jewish spiritual lifestyle that celebrates life and this world, in the here and now. I want to propose techniques to experience the Divinity that permeates and transcends all that exists, sees Judaism and Jewishness as a multifaceted tradition and civilization that is ever evolving, and also embraces science and history. I want to see the real world and all that is in it for what it is and not what my fantasies might crave.

We face many challenges today in terms of fostering a spiritual lifestyle without dogma. So many elements in our world seem polarized and dichotomized. Society in the West is, sadly, very materialistic and often hedonistic. People who gravitate towards religion are often conservative socially, politically, and theologically. I find great depth and beauty in much of Jewish tradition and, simultaneously, in the contemporary secular world. At the same time, there is plenty to criticize in both.

Reb Zalman Schachter-Shalomi, of blessed memory, was fond of speaking of the paradigm shift occurring in the world today and, therefore, necessarily in the world of Judaism too. We are in the midst of change and, therefore, it is not totally clear where we are headed, but change, and ever more rapid change at that, is increasingly part of our lives. If you are in a moving vessel there are many valid perspectives on what is happening. There's the view from someone watching the moving vessel (and at various speeds in relation to that vessel), there's the view from within it, and there's the longer-distance perspective that captures it down the path, which further modifies our perception.

I am committed to a sense of *halakhah*, that is, to Jewish spiritual paths, which, rather than being divinely decreed, are divined by humans (acknowledging that every human vision is subject to the myopia of its age). I find that *halakhah's* orientation of trying to sanctify our daily life is profound. Yet I do not always feel that the decisions rabbis have come to are necessarily those most likely to succeed in sanctifying our daily lives today. These decisions may succeed for some people, but only for a minority, because they do not address the real-life needs of so many in an evolving Jewish society. The creating of codes of Jewish Law like Maimonides' *Mishneh Torah* or Yosef Karo's *Shulkhan Arukh* enable Jewish communities to share common ritual and cultural practices and to feel connected to centuries of Jewish customs and communities, but those practices do not necessarily respond to twenty-first-century challenges. In a way, the codification of Jewish Law has created a petrifying of Jewish practice. There is a danger of having an idolatrous relationship with practices in which the practice becomes more important than one's relationship with the Eternal One. The means become treated as the end—and that is particularly characteristic of an idolatrous relationship.

Our tradition is multifaceted and multivoiced, containing within it numerous opinions expressed through centuries and millennia. What was a minority opinion in the Talmud a millennium and a half ago might very well be much more suited to today's world than it was at the time it was first offered. Unfortunately, very few of us were blessed with the kind of education that enables us to wrestle with the original sources of our tradition.

After experiencing the pleasure of learning traditional texts with people who had a fluency with them, I felt a compelling desire to acquire that kind of comfort with them too. From 1972 to 1975 in graduate school at The Hebrew University in Jerusalem, where I studied Kabbalah, I became increasingly committed to incorporating a fairly radical feminist perspective to the practice of Judaism. I believed it was vital to transcend the patriarchal foundations underlying Judaism as I perceived it all around me and, furthermore, I saw those foundations as keeping Judaism in thrall to a set of beliefs characteristic of the late classical and medieval world. The earliest Jewish feminist writings seemed way too mild to me, for they always seemed to be asking the male power structure/decision makers (that is, the always male rabbis) to acknowledge the justice of their cause and to grant them equal status. They were essentially asking the men with power to voluntarily relinquish their power after possessing it for countless centuries. I couldn't help but ask, why should we grant that power to dole out privilege to those people whom the patriarchal status quo supports? The structure was such that men granted power to each other and might apportion some small token measure to women. Frankly, I found this deeply offensive. But I felt very alone, especially when in the company of men. I continued to love *Yiddishkeit* (Jewishness), but it so clearly needed to change.

Upon returning to the States in August 1975, I remember running into Chabad Hasidim while living in Manhattan, who were trying to engage young people in discussions about Judaism. Some would say that I didn't want to live an Orthodox life because it was harder than not living it. In fact, *"aderaba"* (the opposite is true). In certain ways it's much more difficult to try to forge a path that remains deeply spiritual without some external authority telling one precisely what to do. That is part of our challenge today—forging Jewish spiritual paths that share the passion of the committed, often of the Orthodox, without the ahistorical convictions, the fundamentalism, and the disavowal of science or a belief in pseudo-science and pseudo-history.

Where Are We Headed?

"Lo neda mah na'avod et Adonai ad bo'ehnu shama" ("We won't know how we will worship the Eternal One until we get there"; Exodus 10:26). These words that Moses says to Pharaoh in *Parashat Bo* of Exodus are emblematic of our situation today. We are so much in the midst of change that we cannot know what Judaism will look like one hundred years from now. We're navigating new waters. We need to keep our eyes on the North Star, have a sense of what our goals are, and stay open.

This situation of living in a time of transition is not unique to our days. It's happened many times before, but what is different today is the rapidity of change. We are in an era in which many quantitative changes have led to a qualitative change in the conditions in which we live. Much of the modernism that promised so much in terms of secular spirituality has not lived up to its potential. Art forms have been consumed by consumerism and materialism. Popular music, which in the 1950s and 1960s seemed able to express changing values, has become so commercialized that it has been largely compromised. Many artistic movements seem to have an arc of development: they begin as transformative and even revolutionary, peak, and then play themselves out or become conservative in themselves. Commercialism alone can't be blamed for that, but at the same time the marketing of most art makes it much more prone to catering to a public that is overrun with profit motive, materialism, and fashion.

Psychological Maturity and Spiritual Experience

There's a contemporary Hasidic anecdote that spoke to me when I first encountered it as a young man: When the Hasid was asked, "What comes first, bread and butter or Torah?" his answer was, "First comes bread, then comes Torah, then comes butter." I loved the response, first because it surprised me. I expected one choice or the other. However, the respondent provided a new perspective with which I identified strongly. Well, it wasn't exactly new—a second-century teacher of the era of the Mishna,[1] Rabbi Elazar ben Azariah, is quoted as saying, *"Im ayn kemakh, ayn Torah"* ("If there is no flour, there's no Torah").[2] Without physical sustenance we can't live, but once we have that basic sustenance we need to feed our souls.

Each element of ourselves requires attention and tending—our minds, our emotions, and our psychological health, in addition to our bodies and souls. How rare is the person who matures equally in all of those areas. By "mature" I mean growing towards the full potential that being human entails. Exalting the "spiritual" to the neglect of other components is not a sign of spiritual elevation, but rather a mark of an imbalance.

A person can undergo an overwhelming spiritual experience, but remain psychologically immature. That immaturity will affect how s/he responds to and integrates the spiritual experience into her/his life. Clearly someone who may have a spiritual or religious orientation can also be morally and socially stunted. This seems

---

1. The Mishna was "sealed" around the year 200 CE.
2. *Mishna Pirkei Avot* 3:21 (Ethics of Our Ancestors).

obvious when you see people, even "religious" leaders, who justify violence and intolerance in the name of their religious beliefs.

There's a significant difference between a flash perception that may alter one's worldview and the lifelong attempt to integrate that insight into the way we live day to day. It's a lifelong pursuit to try to mature. Part of the challenge is the difficulty in recognizing our own immaturity. It has been reported that Mark Twain said that when he was fourteen years old his father was so dumb that he could barely stand being seen with him, but when he was twenty one he was amazed to see how much his father had learned in seven years. If someone had told me that I was immature when I was twenty, I would have felt very wounded by the comment. I could not have recognized the truth of it.

A spiritual experience does not occur in a vacuum. It occurs in the context of a person's social, cultural, and historical time. It occurs in the context of our theological beliefs, intellectual understanding, and psychological state. It is possible to have an overwhelming spiritual experience of a very infantilizing deity—not an experience that overwhelms by the vastness of the vision and that makes you feel infinitesimal in the context of the physical and spiritual universes, but one that makes you feel like a child in need of micromanagement or overweening supervision in order to not go hopelessly astray—in other words, a deity that keeps you childlike rather than encourages the independence that maturity requires. There's something comforting in feeling that we're still children and have a loving parent to take care of us—maybe one even more perfectly loving than the ones who actually raised us. Yet there is something truly liberating and empowering about growing into maturity and attaining whatever level of self-sufficiency of which we are capable.

Response and Responsibility

It's a striking commentary that those who had been slaves in Egypt were not able to enter the Promised Land because their slave mentality would always interfere with their ability to create a society of free people. I think that principle pertains in many situations. Now, seventy-plus years after the liberation of Auschwitz, we see young people, less under the shadow of that trauma, able to have their perspective on the world around them not so determined by it.

There are so many components that push their way into the discussion about Jewish spirituality today. There is the survival instinct that holds on to elements of the past even when they no longer serve the function that gave rise to them. Some parts of the Jewish tradition probably owe their continued existence to this, but, on the other hand, tradition also connects you to your ancestors hundreds and even thousands of years ago. Surely there is also a visceral, subconscious element of tradition that speaks to us in ways that may be significant, but not readily comprehensible. This might be comparable to the way certain aromas evoke particular emotions. We feel them, but we don't always grasp why and sometimes don't even recognize that something is affecting us.

There is such a weight to the past in Jewish history that speaking of change can feel disloyal. Our forebears often responded to adversity with the defiance of upholding ancient traditions. People may protest that we should not abandon things for which our ancestors died. I understand the emotion behind those responses, but our spiritual health and clarity should be our priority, especially when certain traditions have outlived their use. This is clearly the case regarding the patriarchal elements of traditional Jewish social structures. Thrown into the mix is also the fact that social cohesion is looser and looser in contemporary society, which makes people cling to parts of the past irrationally with the hope of maintaining some connection to their roots.

We are living in the wake of two of the most defining events in all of Jewish history: the Holocaust and the rebirth of the State of Israel. Of course, there have been other incidents of momentous change in Jewish history and Jewish sacred mythology. For example, the destruction of the Second Temple in Jerusalem in 70 CE was followed by the spiritual revolution of Rabbinic Judaism.[3] The

---

3. This is not to say that the earliest precedents of Rabbinic Judaism

onset of modernity also necessitated a dramatic change in Jewish life and spirituality. The various historical forces that precipitated the French revolution catalyzed the Jewish Enlightenment and the separation of Jewishness into religion, nationality, and ethnic identity. Only the technology of modernity could render realizable the dream of Zionism but also make possible the Nazi technology of mass extermination.

Today's technological growth has made instant global communication a commonplace. It harbors enormous power that can potentially make people deeply informed and/or render them more susceptible to the manipulations of others. Technological growth has the ability to release us from drudgery and free us to pursue other, perhaps more spiritual, concerns, but it also can distract us with a myriad of entertainment possibilities of negligible spiritual value. As always, we have the ability to use our tools to create a golden calf or a *mishkan*, a tabernacle.

At the same time that we have greater insight into the workings of the natural world than ever before, we live in societies that are increasingly mechanized and distanced from nature. Instead of awe in the face of nature, we increasingly deface and disrespect it.

Tradition and Postmodernity

Can we embrace a Judaism that draws inspiration, nourishment, and practice from the tradition while advancing contemporary sensibilities of democracy, freedom, and egalitarianism? Though such a question has been answered with an unqualified "yes" by the various liberal denominations of Judaism, the fact remains that the transition from mythologically based spirituality to non-supernaturally grounded spirituality is not an easy one.

It is no wonder that so many Jews, underexposed to the more mystical strands of Judaism, have sought spiritual sustenance outside their own heritage. Others, having been attracted to the fervor and intensity of Hasidism or to various versions of Orthodox

---

postdate the destruction of the Temple, but rather that the utter transformation of Judaism does.

Judaism, have embraced the sophistry of apologetics and/or suppressed their reservations because of the challenges these present.
Can we embrace the grandeur of our tradition without sac-
rificing our critical faculties or the achievements of contemporary
sensibilities? Can we affirm and enhance the depth of spirit re-
siding in our contemporary secular life while still celebrating and
learning from the timeless teachings of our tradition? I believe that
we can live passionately and compassionately in the sacred now.

Judaism in Motion

As a teenager I was very committed both to the Jewish tradition
and Jewish spirituality and to the counterculture of the 1960s. They
coexisted comfortably within me, though to the outside observer
they may have appeared incongruous. Nevertheless, I was deeply
fed by both. Though always interested in what other spiritual traditions were about, especially in their mystical streams, I found all
the sustenance I needed in my own tradition.

It was painful to see how alienated so many of my contemporaries were from the spiritual traditions of their ancestors and
to watch so many of the more spiritually attuned ignore their
own roots or be unaware of them and their riches. They had so
much to offer Judaism and vice versa, but the spiritual poverty
they perceived in synagogues chased them away. Young Israel of
Sunnyside, Queens, was in certain ways a European synagogue,
that is, many of the adult congregants of my parents' generation
were European refugees and retained many of the customs of their
past. They retained what they would have called a *"yiddishe ta'am"*
(literally, a Yiddish, or Jewish, flavor).

Possibly the fact that Young Israel was located in an urban,
working-class/lower-middle-class neighborhood with a largely
first-generation American Jewish membership made it less prone
to the characteristics of suburban synagogues of which so many
of my peers complained. There remained a strong emotionality in
the place with which I was very comfortable. The Polish Jewish
refugees among whom I was raised (that is, my parents and most

11

of their friends) always seemed much more intensely emotional than the American Jews I knew. My parents and their friends generally had grown up in Jewishly observant homes, but had left that behind in Poland. Their identity, however, was clear and included a strong emotional attachment to the Judaism of their parents, none of whom survived the War. I was not the only child to have no grandparents. None of the children of my parents' friends had them. That was normal to me.

My experience and that of my parents is disappearing. I think about how not only their voices, but the very accent that characterized the way in which they spoke will soon cease to be heard. Similarly we have to recognize that whatever the primary experiences that forged our identities and worldviews were, they are unavailable to the succeeding generations. Those generations will have their own formative experiences. Society is perpetually evolving. Being blind to that evolution is a dead end that ultimately renders us irrelevant to all but those who are similarly blind. To think we have no influence over our evolution, however, is a dangerous error.

What I am suggesting is that we have to recognize a Judaism in motion. As it is written in Leviticus 19:32, "*mipnay sayva takum*," which is usually understood as "rise [in respect] before the elderly." We can also read this as "rise before [you become] [old or] aged [in your ways]." It is spiritually healthy to recognize that growth is essential and change inevitable. Of course, not all change is growth or improvement upon what has been replaced. Some elements evolve sooner or later than others, so periods of change, like our own, always entail uneven, disorienting transitions.

We can either try to effect change, be affected by change, or some combination of the two. In order to consciously try to effect change we need a coherent philosophy or theology. In the past, philosophies tended to be all-encompassing worldviews, but the increasing complexity of our world and the increasing impossibility of attaining mastery in more than one field has tended to narrow the scope of thinkers. We also recognize that our insights have a shorter and shorter shelf life over the successive decades.

So, rather than attempt an "ultimate" theology or philosophy, it is reasonable to think of ourselves as moving towards some greater understanding while remaining cognizant that complete understanding is unattainable. But it gives us direction just like a sunrise helps guide us in an easterly direction. As long as there is life, nothing remains static. Our aging, our relationship or proximity to death, and the innumerable components of human and planetary evolution all modify our view of our place in the cosmos and vis-à-vis the Divine.

The Challenge of Change

Because change is inevitable, there is always a danger that any philosophy or theology will calcify and become inflexible and rigid, that it will become a kind of orthodoxy. There are orthodoxies of Reform Judaism, Conservative Judaism, as well as of nominally Orthodox Judaism. Just as what was meaningful and helpful to us in childhood is no longer adequate when we become adolescents or adults, so (if we continue to grow spiritually) we will require spiritual nourishment from different sources or with different emphases. Judaism has so many elements, strands, and components that some may remain vital while others cease to be meaningful to us. This doesn't mean that we should randomly pick and choose, but rather that we should try to study and understand our tradition as best we can and take into account many factors when deciding how to practice.

One of the strengths of traditional Judaism is the strong community of fellow travelers it provides. There's a community that can potentially share your spiritual practices and that also extends throughout centuries and millennia. That's often a strong component in influencing our practices, but what is spiritually meaningful and has a ring of reality and truth to it needs to be central. Whatever choices we make will affect the Judaisms we offer our descendents. Those choices should not be random or whimsical, but should be made as though our lives depend on them. They do.

The question of change and growth applies to individuals, communities, and traditions alike. Even if we accept the beliefs or practices of our ancestors, they cannot possibly mean the same thing to us that they meant to them, because we believe them or practice them in a dramatically different context. Even contemporaries don't necessarily comprehend ideas, beliefs, practices, etc. in the same way. People may keep certain traditions in different manners, or even in the same manner but for different reasons. One of the major fallacies of fundamentalism is the claim that only one true Judaism has ever existed. This is not only historically fanciful, but it is even false in any given time period as well. Fundamentalist Judaism makes the claim that God is the literal source of the one true eternal Judaism. If you don't accept this, but rather see Judaism (and all religions) as a human creation or even divinely inspired, then you hope that it may express our most sublime understanding of reality and existence. That is a lot to strive for.

Transition and the Tradition

The sense that Judaism and Jews have been in a state of crisis is certainly not a new idea. Forty years ago a book called *On Jews and Judaism in Crisis* by Gershom Scholem came out, collecting some of his essays translated into English. The essays were older and the theme itself has probably been in the air since Napoleon granted Jews civil rights and it became possible for Jews to enter the larger society. A little before Napoleon's reign, two major Jewish movements emerged. The influence of both of them is still felt to this very day. They were the Jewish Enlightenment (*Haskalah*, as it's called in Hebrew) and Hasidism, which was then a mystical revivalist movement.

To a significant degree, any Jewish movement since that era that connects to the contemporary world while also attempting to cultivate a serious spirituality will incorporate elements of those two movements. Modern Orthodoxy such as the type taught by Rabbi Joseph Soloveitchik would certainly fit in this category. Soloveitchik spoke of *Torah* and *mada* (Torah and science) as being complementary disciplines rather than contradictory ones. Unfortunately, for the ultra-Orthodox, Torah and science don't coexist comfortably.

Orthodoxy is not synonymous with the Jewish tradition. The tradition is a vast body that contains considerable diversity of thought. It is not the monolith that it is too often portrayed as being. Unfortunately too many Jews lack both a familiarity with the tradition and the tools for making it their own, relying instead on other people's presentation and interpretation of it. Too many of us have abandoned it to the Orthodox or to the clergy of the non-Orthodox denominations.

The non-Orthodox branches of Judaism acknowledge in principle the validity of change. Organic and "authentic" change comes from the voices of the past and the evolving insights of the present giving birth to the next generation. This has allowed Jewish culture to adapt, survive, and even thrive through many transformations. "Judaism in motion" implies a Judaism that has the resilience to remain relevant through the sweeping changes that society undergoes while upholding the tradition's transcendent insights. It further implies commitment to a Judaism practiced out of conviction because it cultivates the spiritual, moral, and social values we uphold and not because it is too inconvenient and demanding to be Orthodox.

Orthodoxy presents a world of seeming absolutes at the expense of a more nuanced understanding. It's comforting to have absolutes, to have ready-made answers that veer away from all the gray areas in life where answers are not so clear cut. However, it requires relinquishing our critical faculties in order to do this. We have to ignore so much scientific information that has been acquired over the centuries. Science doesn't pretend to offer final answers to age-old questions. It understands that future generations will accumulate new information that will surpass the information of the past and the present. When studying historical events "scientifically" we always hope to uncover documents that shed new light on the past. In most fields of study the prevailing understanding is that successive generations will discover new insights to which previous generations were not privy. The Jewish tradition has provided new perspectives by interpreting the ancient scriptures freshly, finding new meanings in the same ancient words. Many times the more Orthodox people believe that those novel understandings have always been there and that they're nothing really new.

Values and Sensibilities

An idea usually contains within it elements that will someday lead to growth beyond the original concept. Let's take, for example, the biblical injunction, "*Tzedek, tzedek tirdof*" ("Justice, justice pursue!"; Deuteronomy 16:20). Our understanding of justice may evolve over time. Today we may understand justice as demanding a restructuring and a redistribution of power and responsibility in the Jewish world that would have been an affront to the rabbinic hierarchy of Talmudic times. Yet we share the core biblical commitment to pursue justice. Similarly, the Greek concept of democracy would not suffice in our world, and our contemporary understanding of democracy may come to appear overly narrow at some future point.

Maybe we are living in our own version of a "pre-Copernican" worldview, but a "post-Copernican" understanding is too far beyond us to have an inkling of the revolutions in perception awaiting humanity. The best we can do is to remain receptive, but not uncritical, to new insights. "*Kushta ka'ey, shikra la ka'ey*" ("The truth stands; a lie will not stand"; Babylonian Talmud, Tractate *Shabbat* 104a).

The ideal of holiness, *kedushah*, is truly central to the Jewish tradition. How does a person acquire a sense of *kedushah?* Is it different from acquiring a sense of beauty or morality? None of these have external, measurable standards. They're not like trying to acquire a skill or information. They can be cultivated to a degree, but what enables someone to perceive beauty in something, for example, is the result of many cultural and personal factors.

Our sensitivity to beauty, morality, and holiness adds dimensions to every lived moment. Moral sensitivity reflects our aptitude for compassion. Compassion reflects our ability to see beyond ourselves with a depth of experience that elicits caring. Dispassion is not an expression of depth of vision; love is. Compassion, love, and moral sensibility are road marks of a richer experience of our lived moments, although they may not always provide tranquility.

There is a popular understanding of the Hebrew sense of *kedushah*, holiness, as implying "set apart," as, for example, *Shabbat* (the Sabbath) is set apart from weekdays, kosher is set apart from *treif* (non-kosher), etc. I would like to suggest a sense of holiness as a state of consciousness that is *separate* from mundane consciousness, a state of consciousness that perceives the Divine in everything and that therefore recognizes the sanctity of all creation. Consequently, acts that cultivate that consciousness and/or live consistently with it are "holy" and those that do not are "profane."

It is the spiritual dimension that sanctifies. We use the words "good" and "evil" when referring to ethical behavior, but what turns ethical behavior into sacred behavior is the Divine consciousness that compels it. Merely reciting a prayer or performing a ritual does not make it sacred. The prayer and ritual may have come into being to provide a framework for sacred consciousness or to be a catalyst for it, but they cannot guarantee it. Mere exposure to works of great beauty cannot guarantee an appreciation of them or the depth to which one is touched by them, which is the aesthetic parallel to compassion.

One can understand spirituality and the sacred in different ways—some are naturalistic and some are supernatural. A naturalistic viewpoint tends towards seeking an experience of the sacred, while a supernatural orientation usually veers towards belief and dogma rather than experience. A naturalistic sense does not see the decree of some heavenly authority as determining what is holy or profane. Rather, it is the state of consciousness that experiences the sacredness of all existence because it partakes of Divinity and this awareness "commands" actions consistent with that awareness. Are our actions life-affirming, compassionate, and loving, or not?

Our understanding of God will largely determine our sense of the sacred. A belief in a god that is king-like or parent-like will produce a sense of the sacred consistent with that view. It will reflect a simple faith that a child or a subject has in a parent's or king's knowledge that is inaccessible to the child or subject.

Though "absolute" knowledge is unattainable, we may have an experience that fills us with a feeling of contact with the Absolute. This sense of contact with the Absolute combines an awareness of the Infinite with a recognition of how limited we and our knowledge truly are.

Consciousness and Ethics

Consciousness is not an idea, a belief, or a thought. It is a state of being, and in that state we naturally experience the world in a way consistent with it. It's analogous to ethical behavior. A person can do the same act for many different reasons. One might do it because of being told that doing it is "good" and not doing it is "bad." It can be done out of a fear of punishment or a hope for reward. All of these reasons are externally motivated. The same act might be motivated by a feeling of love and compassion. Externally there may be no obvious difference between the actions, but internally the distinctions are huge.

In the realm of Mitzvot *beyn adam lakhavero* (between people), the end result is what matters. Ethical behavior with no consciousness is preferable to awareness with no consequent action. However in the realm of Mitzvot *beyn adam lamakom* (between humans and the Omnipresent), one's consciousness *is* the point.[4]

Consciousness of God should lead to ethical behavior. The greater one's awareness of the Divine, the more refined one's

4. There are theological positions asserting that God needs our specific actions. This, clearly, would parallel the ethical in which our actions are primary and our consciousness secondary.

ethical sensibilities should be, but the "character" of the Divine "encountered" will largely determine what that looks like. In other words, if someone believes they have an awareness of a vengeful god who demands violent, punitive behavior from his faithful, this will likely result in behavior we normally don't think of as ethical. Conversely, our connection to a sense of holiness and a reverence for life, our perception of God pervading all creation and creatures, should be reflected in highly ethical behavior.

A sense of holiness is not always a perception, but often a belief. Just as people believe in the existence of God, people also believe that certain objects, actions, etc. are holy. Other people *experience* objects or actions as holy. They have an awareness of a level of existence that transcends the mundane and transforms it into another level of being. Such experiences can remain in a person's awareness, even when they no longer actively perceive the world with that heightened awareness.

The Torah says, "*veh'yitem k'doshim lelohaykhem*" ("you shall be holy to your God"; Numbers 15:40). What does it mean for a person to be "holy"? I believe it means to live with an awareness of Divinity pervading and encompassing all that exists (what the Zohar calls "*m'malei kol almin*" and "*sovev kol almin*") and behaving in a manner consistent with that awareness. Another aspect of "being holy" is to live in such a way that your life enhances other people's awareness of *kedusha*, of holiness. If you behave in a way that deeply respects another person, people who witness it will recognize that and be positively affected by it. Likewise, if you perform a ritual with a sense of devotion and consciousness, other people may be touched by it and cognizant of that level of engagement. The ritual may acquire greater meaning for them. At a minimum, "being holy" connotes not living on the level of externality, but rather relating to the spiritual dimension of things. It means living in a way that embodies and catalyzes this awareness—living in a life-affirming way that helps others see the sacredness in all existence. *Kedusha* is a level of consciousness and consequent action towards which we should always strive, while having compassion towards ourselves and others in our failures to attain it.

The Sacred and the Secular

People who don't live "religiously" centered lives can have an equally powerful sense of holiness. They may not necessarily use that word to describe their reverence, but that doesn't negate what they actually experience and how they act. Many early secular Zionists, for example, clearly saw working the land of Israel as a life-affirming and sacred act. On the other hand, preaching "holiness" doesn't guarantee that one truly experiences it. In fact, it is often the hollowness (rather than the hallowedness) of the language of holiness that alienates spiritual secularists from traditional "religious" paths. They may reject religion because it has demeaned spirituality in their eyes and because it too often has lacked a sacred sense of people's daily secular existence and can even tend to thwart the life-affirming energies with which people are blessed.

To perceive life as a sacred journey and to witness the spiritual core that sustains all existence doesn't require a formal religious tradition. In fact, it often seems that formal religious training can blunt that very sensibility. How often have we seen people in positions of religious authority who seem oblivious to and alienated from the glories of the physical universe and the spirit that enlivens it? At the same time, it is difficult to pass on to succeeding generations a sensitivity to the spiritual dimension underlying all existence. The Jewish tradition is constantly concerned with teaching our children both verbally and viscerally through ritual activity and the study of sacred text.

How should we engage sacred texts from the perspective of "Judaism in motion"? Sacred texts are not sacred because of their historical accuracy, but because of their ability to convey and catalyze spiritual insight. They need not be "flawless" in some literal, logical manner. The need to see them as flawless, in fact, devalues them by reducing them to the state of literal truth. That may sound like a contradiction, but it isn't.

There is no one correct reading of a sacred text. Different readings are meaningful for different levels of consciousness. "Meaningful" is not synonymous with "true," though the two clearly may overlap. Something may be historically inaccurate yet remain "meaningful." It may possess a different kind of truth that speaks insightfully of spiritual, emotional, or psychological states despite being inaccurate on the literal, historical level. This reminds me of Walt Whitman's lines in canto 51 of "Song of Myself": "Do I contradict myself? / Very well then. . . . I contradict myself; / I am large. . . . I contain multitudes."

The tradition asserts that the Torah "speaks in the language of humans" (Babylonian Talmud, Tractate *Brakhot* 31a). It tries to convey through the medium of language something that language can never fully convey. The closer language comes to the core of spiritual experience, the more it must be satisfied with pointing towards what it's trying to communicate rather than being able to adequately express it. Poetry is that use of language that tries to push verbal expression to its limits, that tries to transcend the limits of language. Metaphor and symbol and various musical elements of language all contribute to poetry's attempt to communicate beyond the limits of rational discourse. Rational discourse is a great tool for communicating facts and for critical thinking, but non-rational thought, thought that is not linear but rather tries to convey more holistic, multidimensional perceptions, requires the rich language of poetry. When one confuses this type of language with linear, literal language you descend into fundamentalism and contract your consciousness instead of expanding it.

The Literal and the Ineffable

Once a person has been touched by the One who pervades and encompasses all, the *m'malei kol almin v'sovev kol almin*, the language of paradox and metaphor becomes a necessary tool for attempting to express that experience. No language is up to the task, but anything less is woefully inadequate. Of course this doesn't mean that people to whom such an encounter is not real have no meaningful connection to sacred writings. Different readings are valid and meaningful for different states of consciousness.

The further one's connection to the Divine is from the Ineffable, the more literal will be one's reading of sacred text and the more one will feel that this reading is definitive, rather than one of many. The more we make God in our own image and the more God is seen to act in accordance with the model of humans, the more constricted is our ability to tolerate a multiplicity of readings of sacred text. That's why I find the statement in Midrash *Bemidbar Rabba* 13 "[There are] seventy faces to the Torah" so powerful. Again, seventy is not meant to be taken literally, but rather seventy is a number that implies a great many.

To someone seeking a connection to the Ineffable Transcendent One, a literal reading of sacred writing will sound absurdly off the mark. An interpretive tool like *gematria* (which uses the numerical equivalents of the letters of the Hebrew alphabet to uncover hidden connections between words and phrases and hidden meanings of scripture), however, can catapult you out of the linear mode of thinking. The language of *gematria* is the language of the trans-logical. If you try to take *gematria* literally, at face value, it will appear ludicrous to most people because that's not the appropriate way of relating to it. Interpreting a text with the use of *gematria* does not negate the existence of a "*pshat*" (a historical, literal denotation), but that is more the concern of the fundamentalist at one end of the spectrum and the historian on the other. If you seek a living relationship with the *m'malei kol almin* and *sovev kol almin*, it is not accessible in that kind of reading. A mostly anthropomorphic god is audible on that frequency. To reach a deeper level we need to hear in another way. We need to be able to turn *ra'ash* (*resh, ayin, shin*), "noise," into a *sha'ar* (*shin, ayin, resh*), a "gateway" to the Divine through our hearing. We are listening to the same thing in both states, but one way of deeply hearing turns it into a *sha'ar*, a gateway, and another is stuck with *ra'ash*, noise.

The root of *sh'ma* (*shin, mem, ayin*), "hear," also means to understand, as in the expression "*na'aseh v'nishma*" ("we will do and we will understand"; Exodus 24:7). When you truly can hear, you are already understanding on a certain level. Traditional postbiblical texts are generally peppered with proof texts read or reread in such a manner as to confirm and corroborate the author's view. Just as we are reading scripture with an eye towards inspiration and a gateway to Divine consciousness, proof texts affirm that this vision and sensibility exists in the canon of Jewish sacred writing.

Judaism is a tradition of the sacred word. The Mishna (*Pirkei Avot* 5:1), summarizing the account of creation that opens the book of Genesis, says that the universe was created via ten Divine utterances, that is, by means of Divine speech. What would make the phrase "Divine speech" comprehensible if we do not believe in an anthropomorphic deity?

Words when spoken can have great power, though they lack all physical form. Just like the various words for "soul" in Hebrew, that is, *neshama, ruakh, nefesh,* which all have to do with breath, spoken words express something whose power is palpable but whose presence is invisible.

All words of Torah are words that humans can string together. Their holiness is dependent upon the consciousness infused in them and the consciousness with which we perceive them, or, in other words, in our ability to perceive or connect to Divinity by means of these words. Personally, certain words of Torah are profoundly moving and inspiring to me, while others are far from that. The same Torah contains the sublimity of Jacob's spiritual awakening when he dreams of the ladder with its "head in the heavens" and the low-consciousness command to stone to death someone for certain transgressions like not honoring Shabbat.

The *kavana,* the intention, with which we invest something, determines its sanctity. Gold was used in forging the golden calf and in the construction of the *mishkan,* the Tabernacle. At all times we may be engaged in the construction of a *mishkan,* a tabernacle, or at the other extreme, a golden calf. Our moment-to-moment choices of how we act and how we speak affect our current as well as our future consciousness. We use the same basic tools in the construction of both. It is a perennial choice whether we cultivate our spiritual potential or not.

God and Spirituality

The realm of the spiritual covers a broad spectrum of human consciousness and is not the monopoly of the God oriented. Our understanding of God, of course, will influence how we view our spirituality. As the great Hasidic teacher Levi Yitzchak of Berditchev (1740–1809) said to the *Maskil* (adherent of the Jewish Enlightenment), "The God you don't believe in, I don't believe in either."

Every act and moment in our lives has a spiritual dimension, just as it has an emotional and psychological dimension. The spiritual dimension may be pervaded by an awareness and sensitivity to the Divine, but it also may not. Within either of those broad possibilities there are innumerable further possibilities that are affected by our experience and understanding of God. It is not uncommon that "religious" training impedes someone's connection with the Divine because that training has imposed an understanding of God that is incongruous with the person's experience of the world. In such circumstances, a person may still have profound spiritual experiences yet find the term "God" unhelpful in describing or assimilating them.

It is my hope that we may help build a *mishkan* and not a golden calf. Which practices may facilitate our spiritual growth and insight and which may inhibit or undermine them will be discussed in subsequent chapters.

Chapter 1

Spirituality and Religion

THE SPIRITUAL CONNECTS US to the essence of existence that transcends our momentary sojourn in this world. It connects us with dimensions of life that coexist with our physical and sensory experiences and anchors them in Being. The spiritual releases the eternal in each moment and the universal in each particular. The spiritual sanctifies whatever is present when its quality of presence is palpable. Spirituality is a state of being in, and a way of relating to, the world. Despite external and even communal expressions of it, it tends to be individualistic and inherently private.

In the interface between spirituality and religion, there is the spiritual life that finds itself within an established religious tradition, the spiritual life that overlaps with the domain of an established tradition, and the spiritual life that inhabits a parallel universe. A focus of this book is the fostering of a harmonious and evolving relationship between the "received wisdom" of the Jewish tradition and the "perceived wisdom" of the one engaged in this journey.[1]

Most examinations of the spiritual are so subjective that the entire enterprise is very slippery. Our cultural, historical, and ideological biases are often camouflaged, but they're embedded in our understanding and communication. The challenge of

---

1. "Perceived" here denotes what a person believes s/he experiences as opposed to implying a contrast with reality.

communicating spiritual experience is comparable to articulating the experience of love. Someone may have an overwhelming experience of love but lack the ability to articulate the very emotions so powerfully felt. This doesn't negate the reality of the experience.

There are innumerable experiences of love and similarly there are countless kinds of spiritual experiences. We commonly use the terms "spiritual" or "love" with no guarantee that we are talking about identical experiences. What the "reality" behind our subjective experiences is goes beyond our abilities to verify. Whatever we can "measure," that is, be objective about, will always remain extraneous to the essence of these life-changing experiences. Yet, despite these limitations, we recognize the realm of love and that of spiritual experiences.

Judaism and Spirituality

I want to be explicit about a few "givens" when writing about religion and spirituality. How spirituality and religion interrelate varies with respect to each individual religion, its branches, and the multiple orientations of their practitioners. Judaism is not monolithic, even within its particular branches. Judaism has a history and an evolution. Biblical Judaism's relationship to spirituality is not identical with Talmudic, medieval, or contemporary Judaism's relationship to it. Even within any of these epochs, there are numerous voices. In rabbinic times, the sensibilities of Hillel and Shammai were distinct, as were those of Avraham Abulafia and Rashi during medieval days.

Generally speaking, in the past at least, people exposed to a particular set of beliefs tended to adhere to them, whereas people in another part of the world, in a different culture, believe with comparable conviction in a different set of beliefs. On the other hand, people who believe in a supernaturally revealed tradition have less difficulty with this issue. They believe they have the one "truth," a truth that is not subject to verification, but rather subject only to the apologetics of believers in their specific supernatural revelation.

Of course, there is no such thing as "generic" spirituality or religion. There are no generic scriptures, generic experiences, or generic humans, obviously. However, there are enough common qualities and characteristics in each that enable us to speak in broader and more general terms.

All religions exist and evolve within specific social, cultural, and historical contexts and there is a relationship of reactions to and effects upon these factors. The particular ways in which any religion survives or thrives in its milieu is unique: its various branches have their own manner of operating in the historical moment and their own relationship with the environment. Generally speaking, the more a religion is "established" in a society, the more it tends to strike a deal with the values of that society. This is true even of religions such as some branches of Judaism that do not attempt to integrate with their host society. The religious establishment becomes a player in upholding the society's values. When disharmony develops between the society's evolving values and the religion's more slowly evolving ones, religious establishments, like all establishments, tend to treat as sacrosanct the prevailing conditions in which they thrive and thus come to form a conservative lobby in an evolving society. This can occur even though the religion's origins may have been quite radical.

We cannot minimize the socializing, organizing, and controlling elements that are part of the fabric of organized religion. Though society requires organization, the conservative presence of religious establishments generally inhibits growth, whether social, cultural, or spiritual. I do not mean to imply that religion in itself is inherently an inhibiting force, but once it becomes structured as an established organized presence it tends to treat its status quo as sacrosanct and tries to stifle change.

At the same time, religions generally incorporate some response to a sense of awe and spiritual awareness. Subsequently they attempt to domesticate that awe and awareness within the framework of the society in which they are integrated. Domesticating the raw spiritual experience dilutes its impact. The raw spiritual encounter often has the impact that the poet Rilke expressed in

27

the conclusion of his poem "Archaic Torso of Apollo": "You must change your life." Spirituality, especially mystically oriented spirituality, tends to become a vestigial presence the greater the "success" of the organized religion in becoming part of the mainstream of society. The fate of the spiritual foundation of a religion is generally bound to the marginality of the religion because societies, by their nature, require a self-preservative conservatism, whereas the inchoate spiritual sensibility is inherently undomesticated.

The more a particular religion becomes part of a society's conservative infrastructure, the more it tends to eviscerate the mystical and/or spiritual core of the religion. Let me give an example. We in the Western world live in a highly industrialized, consumer-oriented society. A spiritual orientation tends to be much less materialistic. There's bound to be an inner tension between the non-materialistic attitudes of a spiritual worldview and the materialism that sustains our way of life here in the Western world. The society can tolerate a minority of spiritually or mystically oriented people, but it probably could not sustain itself if the proportion of those seekers grew too great. Since the origin of religions tends to come from spiritual depths, the term "spiritual" itself is still valued, though the word's meaning may have drifted very far from the earlier usages of the term. In other words, we may still use the same word because of its emotional weight, but it no longer means what it once meant. It's lost its teeth.

Revelation and Organized Religion

Religions do not all follow predictable, prescribed trajectories. There are many strands in a religion at all times in its evolution. Among these is the powerful response to the experience of revelation. By "revelation" I mean the surfacing, to one degree or another, of the spiritual underpinning of all existence. This is not a conventional understanding of the term "revelation." "Revelation" more commonly implies some sense of Divinity being revealed to people (as to the Jewish people at the foot of Mount Sinai as described in the Torah) or to a particular person. A revelation of this nature could be that of an anthropomorphic deity. Possibly it could be a revelation of the "spiritual underpinning of existence" that is understood by people in an anthropomorphic way. Returning to what remains real and meaningful to me, I can only understand true revelation as some version of glimpsing the One that fills and encompasses everything. This encounter may be largely dormant in an established religion, but it is like an unextinguished ember only needing the right conditions to be inflamed anew. Though its resurrection tends to occur in individuals or small groups, it emanates from too fundamental a part of a person to be suppressed or ignored into extinction.

The shock of this revelation places everything in relief. The familiar world is familiar no longer. Another dimension has suddenly surfaced and become tangible. If one maintains a connection to the experience of God infusing all existence, how could you not crave connecting in the deepest way with all else, feeling compassion for all creatures and seeking justice for them?! How could you not have a sense of affirming all existence and feeling a connection to it (as implied in the reading of the root of the word "*mitzvah*" as deriving from "*tzavta*," that is, being, or consequently bringing, together)? By saying this I'm not trying to gloss over the reality of suffering and injustice in the world. Rather, I recognize another level, simultaneously present, with which injustice and suffering are utterly at odds. But just as we cannot live on bread alone—"*lo al halekhem l'vado yikhye ha'adam*" (Deuteronomy 8:3)—we cannot live on visions alone either. As the contemporary Hasidic anecdote mentioned above goes, "First comes bread, then comes Torah, then comes butter."

Moments of encountering the living Presence of the All-Encompassing One are gloriously disruptive of the status quo. They elicit exultation and/or awe. They cannot be confined to mundane laws or scripted rituals, even those whose origins in the distant past had an eye toward the Divine. After returning to everyday consciousness, these extraordinary moments can still vivify the daily routine if sensitively assimilated into it. The vast structure of traditional Judaism's ritualized activities, the *mitzvot*, which cover so much of life's activities, create a framework within which to do this, but only if a person lives this lifestyle with the necessary *kavana*, that is, with the requisite consciousness. Otherwise the acts become rote and sometimes even empty. Of course, to expect someone to live with this level of awareness all the time is unrealistic, but whatever we can muster is worth a great deal.

The meaning and motive underlying an action or ritual is not static over the course of generations, let alone millennia, but rather evolves along with the conditions of existence. In other words, a particular action may have begun with a specific purpose, but the purpose attached to it can change though the action or ritual may remain the same. It's hard to imagine that the understanding someone in a much more primitive society may have regarding a ritual would be identical with the understanding someone living in an advanced industrial society might have. Even if our contemporary believes s/he shares the understanding of her/his ancient forebear, it's really not possible to completely separate our present awareness of the world from our perception of the ritual. To think we can is totally unrealistic.

Throughout the history of Judaism there have been those who have understood the *mitzvot* as, among other things, catalysts to Divine consciousness. They may have been a minority, such as the Kabbalists, but they model a traditional Jewish lifestyle structured around *mitzvot* as powerful tools for grounding awareness.

The Spiritual Necessity of Structure and Freedom

Ritual needs to both focus and cultivate consciousness while leaving it enough breathing room to thrive and even vivify the tradition. There is always the danger of snuffing the life out of one's spirituality by over-legislating one's life and behavior.

Spirituality is much like creativity, one of its cousins. If you give it a structure, you can help it become more tangible in your life. For example, the sonnet form can provide a structure for poetry, but if you excessively restrict permissible words, thoughts, sentence structures, etc. you may strangle the creative impulse. In the area of the arts we often find a new form of expression comes about by the very necessity to express something beyond the built-in limitations of some inherited or dominant style. The "orthodox" style proves inadequate for voicing new realities, so some innovation occurs out of this inner necessity to express and respond to the changing times. Not surprisingly, the more radical the innovation, the more outraged the public's response.

At some later point what seemed so extreme at first begins to look much less extreme. There's an anecdote regarding a portrait that Picasso painted of Gertrude Stein (this occurred before his much more radical cubist innovations such as seen in his *Les Demoiselles d'Avignon*). Gertrude Stein said, "That doesn't look like me." Picasso responded, "It will."

The balance between structure and freedom requires vigilance. Structure is useful to lend form to the creative energy (or the spiritual encounter) in order to help it have a concrete impact on our lives. When the structure begins to be treated as an end in itself, however, it not only ceases to function as the means to a greater end, but becomes an object of idolatry that cannot coexist with Divine energy and immediacy.

A ritual that may have profoundly embodied some insight, or belief, or helped focus attention on some spiritual concern at one point in its history, may cease to generate that response for various reasons. A person's insight, belief, or perspective may change. The prevalent understanding of life and the universe may have shown the ritual as embodying an outmoded belief. The ritual may remain meaningful to some, or even to many, but the meaning must evolve because so much around it has evolved.

Part of any tradition, clearly, is the conservation of rituals. This conservation over countless generations and the uniformity (or conformity) of custom and practice across centuries and continents exerts a cumulative effect of great power over people's spiritual sensibilities. Unless the spiritual spark has been mostly eradicated from an organized religion, an inevitable tension will persist between the conservative, preservative, prescriptive aspects of the religion and its more radical elements. On the one hand, a religion's power rests heavily in its conservative quarters. This lends it the emotional authority of generations of devotion. On the other hand, because the environment changes (which is increasingly true in our day) the relevance of certain practices may survive more in external form than in inner necessity. If the religion doesn't evolve and be faithful to its most vital traditions, it will cease to remain a living source of, and home for, spirituality.

When the radical elements resurface in an organized religion, they attempt to revitalize the traditions and instill in them a reawakened spirit. This often creates conflict and friction with the establishment that has become the guardian of the faith tradition. In fact, a religion becomes complacent with itself as a "faith tradition" when vital encounters with a Living Presence have receded into legend. Those encounters petrify into stories used more to control than to inspire and people are left with "faith in" rather than "experience of" the Divine.

If we wish to address reality we have to acknowledge that all existence is "in motion." Nothing is static. Even our relationship to the very words we use (and usually think in) evolves. This makes the meaning and significance of rituals or works of art evolve over time. This can be disorienting and frightening. Fundamentalism will often step in and deny all change and decry the world that embraces or accepts change. Fundamentalism authors its own alternative "history" that supports its denial of what more mainstream scholars consider fact. When you know what you want your conclusions to be and your allegiance is to those conclusions rather than to the world as it presents itself, you create pseudo-science, pseudo-history, etc. It does not matter whether the fundamentalists represent a branch of religion or the Bolshevik party—the process of trying to impose a particular viewpoint on the world around you is similar.

You might argue that everyone does this unconsciously. To some degree that may be true, but recognizing this tendency and trying to avoid it is very different from tolerating and rationalizing it.

Tradition as a Means Not an End

Our experiences are subjective. No one else can truly know what we experience. We may even question our own ability to fully understand our experiences. Isn't our own understanding of them itself subjective?

Not all "spiritual" experiences are the same, either in their content or in their effect on the person undergoing them. Though many mystical experiences subjectively attest to one great universal reality, we cannot definitively determine the psychological, emotional, ideological, social, and cultural influences in assimilating and interpreting those experiences. Is it even possible to undergo the same experience in radically different cultural contexts, since the cultural context suffuses the experience?

When someone breaks out of inherited structures, what enables her/him to do so? When there's so much cultural baggage attached to a tradition, how difficult is it to remain committed to that tradition while still giving our ultimate allegiance to God?

If our allegiance is to the Eternal One, then our spiritual connection to the tradition should be as a means and not as an end. Of course the tradition's value is not only spiritual. It has cultural, historical, and sociological value as well as spiritual significance. These other factors will affect a person's commitment to one degree or another. The tradition belongs to those who devote themselves to it. Abandoning it to those who are most stringent in their observance of its practices is not necessarily doing Judaism a favor. Cultivating its spiritual core, on the other hand, *is* doing Judaism and future generations a favor.

Spiritual Maturity

Everything we do affects our consciousness. If we feel committed to being conscious of the Omnipresent One, our words and actions should promote that consciousness and not subtly subvert it. Just as humans evolve from infancy through adolescence into adulthood, and societies evolve through stages in their modes of organization, production, and communication, similarly there is a trajectory of human spirituality. The kingly and paternal imagery that characterize so much of the traditional *siddur* (prayer book) and religious literature reflect their composition during an epoch in which monarchies reigned. There may be people who still find the ancient metaphors meaningful, but treating them as immutable is a form of idolatry, for prayer too is a means, not an end in itself. Kingly and paternal metaphors generally assume a need to appease the father-king, in contrast to metaphors that encourage a union of the individual with an All-Encompassing Divine Presence that does not require us to see ourselves as helpless subjects and/or children.

The maturation of societies and religions occurs at many levels and different stages. There are elements of religion that can nurture and sanctify an individual's spiritual life and growth, and others that function to organize a society and sanction its values and structure. When this sanctioning of a society's structure and values comes into play, a religion's relationship to society is necessarily conservative because the weight of sanctity has been placed upon its institutions. However, individuals don't evolve uniformly. Some people's spiritual lives may be far more (or less) developed than their society's overall spiritual pitch. As a result they may no longer be adequately served and nurtured by their religious tradition, though they may still find benefit in certain aspects of the religion both consciously and unconsciously.

The Art of Prayer

In a traditional Jewish framework, the bottom-line relationship to prayer, for example, is first to be "*yotzei*," to fulfill one's obligation to pray. If someone is preoccupied with being "*yotzei*," then prayer can become an "end" in itself. However, if one is concerned with being "*nikhnas*," that is, deeply entering the experience of prayer, investing it with all of one's being and consciousness, then it remains a "means," a vehicle. Similarly, the particular words of the *t'filot*, the prayers, are also vehicles, rungs on a ladder, threads in a "magic carpet," if you will, to transport our consciousness. Ideally they should facilitate our communing with the Presence, experiencing it, basking in its pervasiveness, feeling its impact in everything, not as a director behind the scenes, but as the animator that fills the animations of the scenes as well, both of which are aspects or faces of the One.

Treating the words of the prayers as more significant than the experience of prayer itself is also *avodah zarah*, idolatry. This does not imply that all words of prayers are interchangeable and immaterial, for the specific words should catalyze one's consciousness. Nor do I mean that all prayer should be improvised and impromptu. Some traditional prayers contain great poetry and, like all art, embody and concentrate great spiritual energy. Editing them irreverently is inappropriate and disrespectful. The language of their original composition was highly charged, often quoting and echoing biblical passages, and too commonly the English substitutions offered in their place lack the original passion and energy.

The traditional prayers are also a repository of the spiritual visions and vitality of our ancestors. On the literal level the words may be antiquated. They may reflect a theology that is no longer ours, but like much great literature they also possess a certain elasticity that enables them to absorb and embody newer meanings. When we dress our thoughts in the language of our ancestors, we can absorb energy beyond our own. The same is true when we find a common language within a community. We both feed the community and are nurtured by it. As with the interrelationship of spirituality and organized religion, the interface between private prayer and communal, scripted prayer requires a balance. The communal energy and ancient overtones of tradition must be balanced with enough wiggle room for the individual consciousness. Every moment exists in the context of all those moments that have anticipated it, but every moment also is the birth of something new. Being sensitive to this inner tension and balancing it well is part of the art of prayer.

A person's orientation towards prayer is primarily determined by what s/he sees it as a vehicle towards. If a person's experience or belief concerning God envisions a father or king that, however benevolent, requires appeasement, then being "*yotzei*," ideally with great conviction, is a completely appropriate attitude. But if this is not one's vision, then being "*yotzei*" seems superficial and beside the point.

A spirituality that finds itself to be radically democratic can only participate in an inherited structure voluntarily, in a way that feels harmonious with one's deepest sensibilities. It can absorb the sense of *mitzvah*, even of feeling commanded, but it sees it through a new filter, a filter that cannot connect to a concept of an omnipotent monarch or parent waiting to dole out punishment or reward. That new filter will depend on how the person understands God and I don't want to imply that there is a one-size-fits-all formula for it.

I find the father/king imagery to be an impediment to connecting to the Eternal One and don't use it at all in my private prayers. Personally it feels very diminishing of God, a very confining inaccurate depiction that reduces reality to its constricted dimensions. For the last thirty-five to forty years in my private *davenen*, my private praying, I have given myself permission to use the *siddur*, the prayer book, as a framework, but to change the words to fit my perceptions of the world. If I did not do that I would not be able to *daven* with the same level of *kavana*. I changed "*melekh ha'olam*" ("king/ruler of the universe") to "*nishmat ha'olam*" ("soul of the universe").[2] That resonates much more deeply for me. I find that when I remove the "*melekh*" (king/ruler) from a prayer or blessing, it feels much deeper for me. In the morning prayer, "*Modeh ani*" ("I am grateful . . ."), for example, instead of "*melekh khai v'kayam*" ("living and enduring ruler") I prefer "*he'khai v'kayam*" ("the living and enduring One"). I do this consistently with all blessings and prayers with one exception these days: the singing of "*Avinu Malkeynu*" ("our Father our King/Ruler) on the High Holidays, which has such intense emotional associations for me that I pretty much give myself up to it. When leading our community in public prayer, however, I

2. A number of years later I encountered people using "*ruakh ha'olam*," which I liked, but since kabbalistically *neshama* is considered a higher level of soul, I thought it was preferable to the use of *ruakh*.

feel the necessity to honor the tradition of the community, whatever it is. When I am the *shaliakh tzibor*, (literally, the representative of the community, that is, the person leading the service), I feel it's my obligation to represent the community with the formulation of the prayers faithful to their traditions.

Responding to God's Presence

Religions generally offer some response to a sense of God's Presence. But does that experience of the Presence demand a response beyond "being" as fully as possible? When the Divinity that fills and embraces everything bursts through into a person's consciousness, other states of awareness pale beside it. How can a person not respond? But what constitutes a genuine response? Must a response express itself externally in action, and if so, in what kind of action?

There can be no prescriptive responses. For some people, the response will express itself in externally recognizable behavior, in others, not. But even in the latter case, the identical behavior may be experienced internally in a vastly different manner. In other words, you might do the same actions, but now your consciousness during those actions is completely changed. For example, you might recite the same prayers and blessings that you said before, but suddenly they mean so much more to you; the words take on a completely different or a much deeper meaning.

It is presumptuous to judge someone else's *kavana* or "spirituality." One can "measure" someone's external adherence to ritual observance, but it reveals little to nothing about the quality of the person's inner life. We cannot attribute spiritual significance to external demonstrations of "religiosity," but rather simply compliance to dogma and ritual behavior.

What about ethical qualities and characteristics? A person can appear to be humble or devoted. Aren't those both internal states with an external component? The truth only exists internally. The appearance may merely be appearance and not go much below the surface. Already in the Talmud (for example, Tractate *Yoma* 72b) we see the expression "*tokho k'varo*" (literally, his "inside" is

37

like his "outside"). In other words, the inside is what truly matters. We esteem people whose outer qualities reflect their inner qualities, but, sadly, that isn't always the case.

We should not confuse a person's level of observance with the vitality of his/her spiritual life. Here again the conservative and radical elements of religion clash. The radical component demands the priority of the inner dimension of all ritual, prayer, etc., while the conservative component places its emphasis on dogmatic and ritual conformity. When *halakhah*, Jewish Law, ceases to be "a way" or "the (traditional) way," but "the (only legitimate) way," it becomes one more idol demanding obedience, commanding that we compel our children to conform to it.

If we say our commitment is to God rather than to *halakhah*, that implies that *halakhah* also must remain a means to the end of connecting to the Divine. When we see *halakhah* expressing and enhancing the greatest insights in our lives "*beyn adam lakhavero*," between ourselves and our fellow humans, then *halakhah* deserves our enthusiastic devotion. When it falls short of our ethical ideals, it should not become a "divinely" sanctioned diminishment of standards. The same, of course, applies to our relationship with the Eternal One and all *halakhot* concerning that relationship. Some people claim that when we perceive flaws in the standards of *halakhah* we don't sufficiently grasp them. Sometimes this may be true. Other times we may grasp them only too well, but recognize in their place a Torah and *mitzvah* "not far from us, but in our hearts" (Deuteronomy 30:11, 14).

Clearly there is some standard and criteria that we are applying by which we are assessing *halakhah*. If we were to see *halakhah* as purely divinely decreed, then it must be the yardstick by which all other values and actions are measured. There are people who hold that position. They would be willing to say that if the Torah says homosexuality is an abomination, then it must be. They would be willing to say that if the Torah says someone should be stoned to death for transgressing Shabbat, that must be a higher standard than one more lenient. Unfortunately we could go on and on. Granted, *khazal* (our Talmudic sages) had difficulty with these laws too.

If we look at *halakhah* and judge it or even attempt to demonstrate how it fits some ethical or spiritual standard better than any other system, we are tacitly holding another system of determining values as more fundamental than *halakhah*. However, there is an even more essential element that enables us to perceive this issue from a thoroughly different perspective.

Divine "Doing" vs. Divine "Being"

The Orthodox view of *halakhah* not only has the connotation of "the way," but also of "the Divine Will," implying a thinking and volitional process parallel to these human activities. Despite traditional attempts to disclaim any similarity between human processes and Divine ones, a residue remains of fashioning God in our image here. There is a vast spectrum of forms this takes, from crude anthropomorphism to subtle sophistry or apologetics, but the anthropocentrism remains recognizable.

This orientation is heavily invested in perceiving God as active in history, which gives rise to a slew of difficulties that have been a focus of theological attention for millennia. How do we explain the obvious absence of justice in the world, the prospering of transgressors, and the suffering of the righteous and innocent, for example? All of these problems emanate from what amounts to a focus on Divine "doing" rather than on Divine "being." Attention to Divine "doing" camouflages the subtext that creation revolves around human existence.

The Divine "doing" orientation is very at home with the king/ father image of Divinity. (This is equally true for matriarchal Divinity imagery, which modifies the "personality" characteristics, but remains essentially another example of fashioning God in human terms). The monarch or parent is characterized by his/her role and "power" in the world as evidenced by its actions, not by its "being." Qualities of "being" are deduced from its actions.

True focus on Divine "being," however, is a qualitatively different orientation. It changes the meaning of the verb "to be" and expands it to encompass a Consciousness uniting all that is. Suddenly, to say that something exists requires an exclamation point: it is suffused with Divinity; it Exists with a capital E! This is strikingly embodied in the central Hebrew name for God, the *Shem Hameforash*, YHVH, the explicit name, whose root is the verb "to be." The Name contains elements of the past, present, and future tenses of this root. When Moses perceives the burning bush and asks for God's name (which in the Jewish tradition implies an entity's essence), the reply Moses receives is *"Ehyeh asher Ehyeh,"* "I will be that which I will be," that is, Eternal Being and Becoming. Aflame, yet unconsumed, and encountered in a humble bush! How perfect an attempt to depict in one succinct image this consummate Consciousness!!

Even though "being" is an activity of sorts, it is an activity of a qualitatively different nature. A focus on Divine Being modifies our reading of the tradition, both in its ritual expressions and its canonical texts. There's a well-known phrase that comes from the Midrash *Bemidbar Rabbah* 13 that says, *"shiv'im panim latorah,"* "(there are) seventy faces to the Torah." In other words, there are many valid ways of reading the Torah. Recognizing that varying cultural and sociological circumstances make inevitable an evolution in how we comprehend the Torah widens the breadth of legitimate readings.

Text and Reader

There is an inevitable dance between a text and a reader. Reading a text from a printed, bound book is not the same as reading those very same words from a scroll, or hearing them as oral transmission, or reading them on a screen. It is not merely an incidental modification. That which brings a book to us in a printed text brings with it cultural, sociological, technological, and other overtones that are all part of the environment that produces books in print. This, obviously, is equally true of texts on a computer screen, e-reader, or in hand-copied manuscripts. The form in which we encounter the text is a part of the "book" itself. Because we are no longer living in a culture that records its thoughts and history on scrolls, reading the Torah in such a form injects an ancient, unique, and solemn aura to a prayer service. Everyone brings the incalculable components of her/his life into a living relationship with the numerous factors bound up in the "book" we encounter. All this and more is contained in the Lurianic teaching that each soul has its own letter in the Torah.

As we mature, we become increasingly responsible for both our inner being and the greater needs of the community. Responsibility to our inner being is not synonymous with narcissistic self-absorption. Rather, it means that we have to discern our inner states and what direction is needed to nurture and enhance our connection with the Divine. We have to find the balance between the individual and communal needs. Who can know our inner states better than ourselves, if we cultivate our inner eye and ear? But, of course, we must never lose sight of our responsibilities toward the community.

It is written in *Pirkei Avot* 1:6, "*aseh l'kha rav*" ("acquire for yourself a teacher"). This phrase is enhanced when read in conjunction with another passage: (4:1) "*ayzehu khakham? halomed mikol adam*" ("Who is wise? The one who learns from everyone"). This is even truer if we modify it to say not only "from everyone," but "from everything." Everything can be our teacher if we have the wisdom to learn from it. This includes the inner self.

How do we know if our understanding is correct? Part of the maturation process is increasing discernment in addition to openness to the insights of others. All others are our teachers, though the lessons we acquire from them may not be the ones they intended to impart. "*Aseh l'kha rav*," "Make *yourself* your own teacher [too]." Cultivate your insight and sensitivities so that you too become your own teacher. One who learns from everyone (or everything) must include oneself as teacher by observing oneself, by honing an awareness of one's inner states and experiences, so that a person can be one's own teacher along with the innumerable others always available. Whether we elect to relinquish all our decision making to an external authority or consciously acknowledge our own responsibility in decision making, all choices are ultimately always our own.

Radical Religion and Spirituality

It is essentially the more radical (meaning the "root") components of religion that overlap most with spirituality. Someone who lacks a community of like-minded seekers is more likely to founder and have less concrete tools for living a spiritual life to pass on to succeeding generations. As long as we are alive in our bodies, our spirituality is necessarily an embodied one. A religious tradition can provide a framework for anchoring and experiencing the spiritual and transmitting it. A spiritual path divorced from all community also has the danger of veering into the worship of our own experience. Community can temper this tendency.

Does religion and religious ritual liberate the spirit or shackle it? Is liberating the spirit a fundamental goal? Moses is often referred to as "*eved Hashem*" ("servant of God"), in contrast to the earlier state of the Jewish people as servants or slaves of Pharaoh. Are we of necessity slaves to something, whether it is those in power, the intoxication of our illusions or ideals, or the limits of our imaginations or consciousness? Are we slaves to our limited conceptions of the Divine, including the belief that we must indenture ourselves to God? In a manner of speaking, we *are* slaves to all of these things. Only by transcending our previous limitations can we comprehend more clearly the scope of our servitude and how detrimental it might be to our spiritual life.

At the center of the Haggadah traditionally recited at the Passover Seder is the statement that in every generation a person should see her/himself as if s/he had personally exited from Egypt: "*k'ilu hu yatzah mimitzrayim*." The Kabbalists like to reread *Mitzrayim* (Egypt) as "*meitzarim*" (narrow places or narrowness itself), broadening the statement psychologically and symbolically. Hopefully we are always leaving the enslavement and narrowness of our beliefs and comprehension of the Divine and growing in our perception and connection to Being.

The more limited our vision, the more limited our world. Religion and religious ritual do not of themselves either liberate the spirit or shackle it. They do, however, encourage and nurture particular views of the Divine. At one stage in history a ritual may serve to liberate us from the more limited views that it transcends. At a later point it may restrict someone whose consciousness has grown beyond the insight embodied in the ritual. Rituals have some elasticity, however. They can be invested with new and revised meanings. But elasticity is not limitless. Part of what defines its meaning is the individual's and community's *kavana* ("intention" or "consciousness") vis-à-vis the ritual.

There often comes a point when people try to reread, and thus deny, the obvious implications of certain aspects of the tradition. There are those, for example, who apologize for the blatant patriarchal nature of Orthodox Judaism by claiming, for instance, that women's "superior" spiritual stature exempts them from the same ritual obligations and privileges as men. Much has been written debunking these claims; it is unnecessary to take the space here. The point remains: there are limits to one's rereading of the tradition. If we are committed both to God and to the tradition, we may of necessity modify aspects of the tradition in order to remain loyal to our growing vision of the Divine and to the world in which we live. Through this delicate process we may facilitate our religion's continuing ability to nurture the spirit.

The tradition contains within it various voices, some spiritually sublime and morally astute, others, sadly, not. There is no one vast voice audible throughout. In our commitment to authenticity, honesty, morality, and God, we need at times to try to move Judaism in directions that reject the lower consciousness of some of its beliefs and reinforce the aspects that promote more insightful and compassionate ones. This is an affirmation of what we believe in good conscience and in "good faith" to be the grandest aspects of Judaism, and an attempt to raise the less conscious elements beyond their nearsightedness. We do this out of a love of God, humanity, creation, and Judaism itself.

Chapter 2

Revelation and Exodus

THROUGHOUT THE EVOLUTION OF the tradition, most innovations have appeared in the form of reinterpreting the meaning of canonized words and/or amplifying or rereading major concepts. Today we may see these innovations as expressing a greater and/ or an additional truth regardless of the original's apparent meaning. Outside of the Orthodox world we don't require the fiction of apologetics or the attribution of all "Torah" to a historical revelation at Mt. Sinai. We require authenticity and meaningfulness.

In the sphere of sacred myth, revelation and exodus are monumental in their scope and power and are intimately interconnected. All revelation implies an exodus from the consciousness in which we previously existed. Revelation is not simply the spreading of information. If revelation were primarily informational, it would remain relatively superficial. Similarly, if you undergo a purely physical exodus, you may experience relief from oppression, but the oppressed mentality accompanies you wherever you go. Revelation must change the very way we see and experience life. True revelation transforms consciousness.

In *Pirkei Avot* 6:2 we find the striking statement, "*B'khol yom vayom yotzet bat kol mehar khorev*," "Every day a Divine Voice emanates from Mt. Khorev" (Sinai). At any moment, revelation, a deepening of consciousness, is accessible. No matter how we answer the perennial question "*Ayeka?*," "Where are you?" (Genesis

3:9) that God addresses to Adam, the potential to stand at Sinai and experience the Divine Source anew remains perpetually present. We can suddenly live more deeply and "be" in a different place. We can witness the same phenomena and suddenly the Sinai consciousness concealed within peeks through

Our understanding of revelation, like all other things, has a history. Unless we live in a condition of some "ultimate" revelation (if such a thing is possible), we are always in some state of "*Mitzrayim*" (Egypt) or "*meitzarim*," that is, restrictedness and limitation. Each revelation brings us to a new state of limitations, not the comfortable, familiar limitations of our past, but a new landscape with new limitations. With a commitment to deepening our awareness, we will hopefully always grow and undergo an exodus from one manner of "*Mitzrayim*" to another, less constricted one.

Learning to See More Subtly

Everything accessible to our perceptions affects us even if we are not always conscious of it. If we are listening to music and subsequently become absorbed in reading, we might become unaware of the sounds that held our attention moments before. As in the case of a movie soundtrack, this diminished awareness does not mean that the music ceases to affect us. Modify the music and the all-but-inaudible background ambience changes. Modulate the color scheme of a room's walls or furnishings and the person who may not note the change will still experience it unconsciously. This is true for emotional and spiritual presences as well. We may be more or less aware of our spiritual, emotional, and physical environment, and some people are more attuned than others. How do we sensitize ourselves? Our intellect can function as a scout surveying the territory our beings can enter. Paying attention to the world around us and to ourselves as part of that world is an important step. Most important, however, is that we learn to look with new eyes and re-view the universe around us.

Most of us have probably had the experience of unexpectedly seeing something freshly after innumerable encounters. Is there an objective change in the object of our perceptions? No, the change is in the perceiver and in the quality of perceptions. Things hidden to some are in plain view to others. I have often experienced this when looking at paintings. I could be standing there looking at a painting for quite a while and suddenly I see something in it that I hadn't noticed before, despite the fact that I'd been looking at it intently. It has also happened with paintings I've looked at on numerous occasions and suddenly one time I begin to see it differently than I ever had before.

Spiritual experience can transform or modify us at a depth of our being, in contrast to "beliefs," which reside much closer to the surface. We often absorb our tradition's creeds to the point that they can monopolize our vocabulary, influencing the very way we comprehend and assimilate life.

Language, Perception, and Experience

Language is a primary tool in our perception of the world. Our ability to think and to experience the universe is generated, yet also constrained, by language. Linguistic sophistication and dexterity can facilitate subtlety of thought. At the same time, there are also non-linguistic ways in which we think, for example, spatially, musically, aesthetically, emotionally, and spiritually. Elasticity of imagination expands our openness to "frequencies" of experience beyond those within the conventional fields of perception. Imagination is also a very broad term connoting a spectrum of activities. Language and other modes of thought evolve in step with our changing civilization and consequent perceptions. Language is not a hermetically sealed cage. It operates more like invisible and somewhat shifting borders that are difficult to think beyond. At the same time, language contains tools to expand these very borders into new terrain.

Language and the formulation of beliefs can open us up to possible worlds, but if the beliefs are too limited they can curb our ability to experience life's multidimensionality, subtly convincing us of the "flatness" of the world. Judaism, like all religions, uses various means to influence our thought and perceptions, such as sacred text and prayer, symbols, modes of music, patterns of social organization, etc. Some of these means may originate with an intention of stimulating an awareness of God. If they rigidify, however, they evolve into the opposite, restricting consciousness by delegitimizing whatever falls outside its parameters. This does not mean that we cannot gain experience outside of our inherited beliefs. People, especially in multicultural environments, are under the sphere of influence of multiple belief systems, most of which harbor the seeds to grow beyond themselves.

The "*bat kol*" (the Divine Voice, which emanates daily from *khorev*, that is, Sinai*)* speaks in many "languages." We may "hear" it in the waves of the ocean, in the radiance of another's countenance, in the veins of a leaf, in the profile of a mountain range, in the space between words, in the earth under our fingernails, or in the fullness of silence. What matters is not the "vessel" for the Voice, but our ability to perceive it.

Revelation is the peak of all perceptions, but revelation is not static. As *Pirkei Avot* 6:2 implies, it is waiting at every moment, at every turn. It is waiting to suddenly leap out in relief from the world perceived with pedestrian eyes. It is waiting for the eyes of *kedushah* (holiness) to suddenly reperceive the world of *khol* (profane) and recognize the *kedushah* pulsing right beneath the surface, vivifying everything.

Though the essential content of revelation may remain basically the same, how we respond to it varies from generation to generation, and from environment to environment. As everything that surrounds us affects us, however subtly, the colossal porridge of all this input becomes the raw material through which we experience and interpret the world and, ultimately, respond to it. Incorporating all this into our lives demands attention. If some people resonate with the traditional Orthodox formulas and manners of response, that's fine, but a more democratic spirituality respects the genuine and inspired responses of others made *l'shem shamayim* ("for the sake of heaven"). The grand mix of ingredients making up our environment will influence our biases, blind spots, and insights. None of us is unique this way.

Regarding the subject of revelation, a number of crucial questions arise. What is the relationship between revelation and *halakhah*, or the relationship between public and personal revelation? How are we to understand revelations that fundamentally contradict each other, for example, if someone claims to experience a revelation of Jesus as Savior or Divine Being in contradistinction to all beings possessing Divinity?

There are many manifestations of revelation. While maintaining that democracy fundamentally respects human dignity and equality, and that one cannot countenance non-democratic forms of government as valid, nevertheless, a democratic spirituality does not connote an "all is equal" view of all paths.

Religious traditions harbor multiple perceptions of revelation and Divinity. So too with Judaism, despite attempts to treat it as a homogenous monolith. Perceptions and conceptions of Divinity and revelation have a history. If Judaism is to continue to thrive, it will persist in forging a history and not act as though that history concluded 250 years ago, or 3,300 years ago, or tomorrow.

A traditional view of revelation is that it occurred to the Jewish people approximately 3,300 years ago with the giving of the Torah at Mt. Sinai, and that *halakhah* constitutes the lifestyle that conforms faithfully to the content of that revelation. The mystical streams within Judaism, in contrast, saw *halakhah* as both an outgrowth of, and a path back to, a new experience of revelation. Furthermore, all "new revelation" was understood as either explicitly or implicitly inherent in that initial revelation at Sinai.

Another viewpoint is that in the messianic age *halakhah* will change. One Kabbalistic formulation explains that although today we read the Torah of the black letters, with the coming of the Messiah we will read the Torah of white letters (the spaces within and between the black letters). A comparable teaching is that now we live according to the Torah derived from the Tree of the Knowledge of Good and Evil, abundant with expressions of "Thou shalt" and "Thou shalt not," but in the messianic era we will live according to the Torah that derives from the Tree of Life. All of these views, however radical, retain the sense of the primacy of traditional *halakhah*.

Halakhah and Evolving Awareness

A traditional explanation for why the generation that was freed from Egypt could not enter the Promised Land of Israel is that since they were raised as slaves, they were not prepared to build a new society founded upon freedom. Their perspective on the world was too constricted, having grown up looking at it through the eyes of slavery. In the Torah, when the twelve spies entered the Promised Land, only two of them (Joshua and Caleb) could see it from a non-constricted perspective and, therefore, only those two could ultimately enter the land.

This is analogous to our situation today. One particular *"Mitzrayim"* that certain fervent adherents of our tradition remain loyal to is the *Mitzrayim*, the narrowness, of sexism. Just as our ancestors saw the uncertainties of the desert as worse than the certainties of a life of slavery in *Mitzrayim* ("better to be slaves in *Mitzrayim* than to die in the wilderness"; Exodus 14:12), so they remain committed to a narrower sense of *mitzvot beyn adam lakhavero* (between humans).

A growing number of people, in their devotion to *mitzvot beyn adam lakhavero*, cannot countenance those practices that seem blind to inequalities between men and women, between heterosexual and homosexual or bisexual, etc. and, therefore, see them as antiquated and at times even a *"shonda,"* an embarrassment. We have experienced a widening of awareness that does not allow us to pay loyalty to specific *halakhot* that offend that consciousness.

We may not always know where a new consciousness will lead us. Though it broadens our perspective, in this case regarding *mitzvot* between people, it doesn't come with imperative *halakhot*, but rather with an imperative to re-vision *halakhot* according to the new awareness. This doesn't invalidate *halakhah* per se, but it does insist that it be scrutinized with this evolving insight. For how can we expect *halakhah* to serve as a vehicle to God or to a grander encounter with the Divine if it transgresses a basic reverence for the equality of all humans? Otherwise *halakhah* becomes another petrified idol demanding an allegiance greater than to the Divine and to the right of all humans to grow unfettered by nearsighted and oppressive social mores. People can still discover and encounter the Divine under conditions of oppression, but those conditions will usually make it difficult to nurture the insights that come from such encounters.

Optimally we need balance and harmony between the spheres of *beyn adam lamakom* (between humans and the Omnipresent One) and *beyn adam lakhavero* (between humans themselves). Experiencing the Divine as encompassing all and filling all existence should compel us to seek justice. However, this does not guarantee that when we attempt to translate our vision into concrete actions, customs, and laws, our unrecognized biases won't lead us to new nearsighted conclusions.

Though it makes sense to seek harmony between all the components of our life, people's sensibilities and faculties don't develop uniformly. Generally some aspects of a person flower disproportionately to others. It is possible that a person (and therefore a community and even a culture) may have a relatively sensitive perception of the macrocosm, but be underdeveloped in her/his sensitivity to the microcosm, or vice versa. We might expect that the greater the sense a person has of the All-Encompassing, All-Embracing One, the greater that person's love of all beings would be. Yet it's not unusual to find people who "devote" themselves to the "Divine" and yet simultaneously persecute others who don't share their devotion or "object" of devotion. Though such people must have a seriously limited sense of the Divine, this doesn't mean that people with a narrower sense of God deserve less human respect. But we cannot "honor" people who persecute others in the name of their beliefs. Persecution in the name of God or religion is no less persecution than if it were cloaked in any other guise.

Coercion and Consciousness

For ritual practices to function as powerful tools for cultivating a consciousness of the Eternal requires, generally, an intimate familiarity with the rituals themselves. This does not come easily. Rarely nowadays, at the very least outside of an Orthodox framework, do "liberal" Jews acquire sufficient Hebrew fluency to be able to make the language the potent tool that it can be. It is rare to find a community of practitioners in the liberal Jewish world who combine a commitment to Jewish practice with progressive ideals. This kind of community exists in liberal seminaries, Ramah camps, college Hillel houses, some places in Israel, and in a few synagogues in major cities.

In order to optimize the usefulness of a ritual (including prayer), it needs to become like a part of your body, which you then can exercise. In a way it is similar to playing an instrument. In order to make great music, you usually have to practice your instrument until it becomes an extension of yourself. Then you can either play the beautiful compositions that others have created or possibly author your own. For someone to devote her/himself to learning an instrument s/he usually needs to see the example of other people making beautiful music with the instrument just to know the possibilities that exist. To make our instrument our own, we need to acquire a level of proficiency. The same is true with the Jewish tradition. Then it can become a great practice for cultivating consciousness.

Freely acquired, consciousness and *kavana* transform everything they encounter. But what kind of consciousness and *kavana* can be forged by coercion? The body may conform to certain rules and regulations, but the mind and consciousness is being suffocated and strangled. A deeper connection with, and experience of, God is being stifled.

The implications of this are significant. A person's growth is stunted if she or he lacks the freedom to grow unhampered. There is a difference between guidance and coercion. Someone with greater experience, knowledge, or insight can provide useful guidance to the less experienced, but compelling the beliefs and behavior of a person stunts inner growth, whether psychologically or spiritually. The analogy between a person's growth into adulthood and one's inner growth into spiritual "adulthood" is relevant.

When we're infants or children, we require considerable external protections and limits to foster healthy growth. As we mature, we thrive from proportionately greater and greater self-determination. The healthier a person's development has been, the clearer their self-directed path will be, because they will not feel compelled to force their inner lives to conform to external expectations. A tree will grow more fully if it has the freedom to thrive. If its roots and its light are greatly restricted, it will contort itself in order to seek more light and room to grow. We are no different.

Just as individuals grow through certain stages physically (for example, infancy, adolescence, and adulthood), they do so psychologically and spiritually as well. On a grander scale, so do societies. Greatly oversimplifying the process, we can say that technological growth enabled societies to evolve such that a widening cross section of people could actively participate in influencing society's structure. For instance, the printing press enabled information and ideas to be more widely disseminated. As a result of this and other developments, the educated classes expanded beyond the elite, giving more and more people greater and greater means for self-rule, leading to demands for increased representation in decision making.

Comparably, one's spiritual self evolves in conjunction with, and in the context of, one's emotional, psychological, and intellectual self. This is equally true for every aspect of a person. In other words, one's emotional life is influenced by one's intellectual, psychological, and spiritual life, etc. Not all change is growth, of course. Our insight can shrink; our vision can darken. Often the very same tool that serves to open someone up can close her/him off. A certain discipline can provide someone the necessary focus through which they thrive, while in other conditions it can squelch someone's creativity or spirituality.

Adversity is a form of external limitation that can catalyze growth when we confront it. We can grow even if we don't triumph over adversity. The natural vicissitudes of life alone provide countless challenges without having to live under the constrictions of some authoritarian figure. Yet the desire to be taken care of, provided for, and nurtured by some powerful parental figure can remain very strong. In the face of our mortality, in the face of the unpredictability of life, how comforting it is to believe in the protection of a parent or lord who will care for us if we are obedient to the rules of the kingdom! That's very much the analog of a child's perspective towards his/her parents, particularly, traditionally, the father. And what is the most powerful human image of such omnipotence? A great king.

Spiritual Empowerment and Disempowerment

When God becomes the King of the Kings of Kings *(melekh malkhei hamlakhim)* and we see our relationship to the Divine as accepting the *"ol malkhut shamayim"* (the yoke of the kingdom of heaven), we are imbibing a metaphor that is highly disempowering. It does not enable us to overcome our ego and idolatry of self when we see the Divine as a super-parent, superimposing upon God the characteristics of ego. In this very limited understanding, *"bittul hayesh"* (the transcendence or annihilation of the ego) becomes the subservience of the human ego to a greater, "higher" ego, which is, essentially, a projection upon God of a glorified version of our own flawed image.

Though different aspects of a person develop at different rates, each aspect affects the ability and direction of development in every other aspect. Someone who is stunted emotionally and psychologically will be more limited spiritually than they would otherwise be. Their emotional and psychological makeup curtails their ability to see certain things clearly because they perceive them through the distorted lens of their limitations.

A metaphor such as the "yoke of the kingdom of heaven" cultivates an anthropomorphic and disenfranchising orientation towards God. It fosters the perception of a "smaller," pettier god, a god with personality (unless we "protect" God's "personality" with the smokescreen of impenetrability or incomprehensibility). Whether this deity is angry, pleased, or generous, it's a colossal diminution to attribute personality traits and human-like motives to God. This brand of deity operates like us, only on a much grander scale, and thus the supernatural and the performance of miracles are the trademark and "calling card" of such a deity.

The perception of existence itself and "being" as "miraculous" is a far more sublime state than a belief in supernatural "miracles." Though it may have a strong impact emotionally, the belief in supernatural miracles touches superficial realms of a person's consciousness. Perceiving life and existence as miraculous (not merely believing it to be, but experiencing it as such), however, expresses a deepening of a person's ability to see. In these circumstances, a person is sensing another dimension of existence.

Faith in miracles does not develop the sensibilities to live more fully connected to God. The greater the emphasis on "belief," and the "supernatural" as a buttress for belief, the stronger the unspoken message that God is inaccessible and we are like children who, in order to earn the approval of the divine parent, must follow a set of rules and regulations, some of which make sense and others of which lack all connection to reason. In a scenario like that, the arbitrariness of the rules is immaterial; what matters is the person's obedience and subservience.

There is a subtle distinction operating here. We may forever find elements of life wondrous and beyond our comprehension. This is part of the rich fabric of human existence. However, if we take that sense and exploit it to justify the incomprehensibility of certain ritualistic regulations, something different is occurring. Claiming that certain practices are inherently incomprehensible is an attempt to place them beyond critical reason. It is reasonable to expect that we may not understand the origins of practices that began millennia ago. For some of these practices, we may have explanations or justifications that were committed to writing many centuries after the practices themselves began. It is also likely that a practice that continues over thousands of years may begin for one reason (or even many reasons) and may later acquire a different reason or set of reasons over the course of centuries. We may decide that the element of tradition alone suffices to justify continuing to practice certain rituals, and that connection to our ancestors is reason enough.

There are many ways to approach the purpose of the *mitzvot*. In fact, there's a whole body of traditional literature devoted to *"ta'amei hamitzvot,"* (the meanings of, and reasons for, the *mitzvot*). We can see *mitzvot* as a means to help us sanctify our daily lives and/or transcend the limits of rational thinking, in order to enter a realm of "intelligent" or conscious being. From such a vantage point the rationality or comprehensibility of each *mitzvah* is less consequential. On its surface the particular *mitzvah* may make no apparent sense. It may have its origins in some primordial or prerational vision or superstition. However, currently it may facilitate a change in awareness of the Divine, rendering the *mitzvah*'s historical genesis as curious, but beside the point. This is not disempowering if the *mitzvah* is seen as a means towards a greater end, that is, a consciousness of the Divine. Yet the very same *mitzvah*, when seen as an end in itself, divinely dictated and impenetrable, becomes part of a structure that disempowers people. It is parallel to the child's view that the parent is omniscient and omnipotent, and therefore her/his control of the child may be incomprehensible, but not without justice.

The Role of Reason

The role of reason in life, including one's spiritual life, is multitiered. No aspect of ourselves exists in isolation from all the other aspects of ourselves. There is a constant interconnection of each aspect with every other; and all are crucial to the health and fullness of being of the individual. "Natural" limitations to our growth potential exist in any sphere, analogous to the example of different kinds of trees being capable of growing only so much, even under ideal conditions. Our intellects are limited, our emotional makeups are challenging, and our spiritual constitution, which can merge with what feels infinite, nevertheless returns to the limits of our individuality over time. The love we may experience as boundless coexists with other emotional realities of life on the physical plane.

How, then, do we employ our rationality and reason, which are such powerful tools? Do we use them to divine and pursue truth, or to "prove" a predetermined point? The ideal of Western philosophy, whose original meaning stems from the Greek words for love (*"philo"*) of wisdom (*"sophia"*), is clearly that reason must be employed in the unprejudiced pursuit of truth. Believing in this ideal does not, of course, guarantee our ability to realize it.

There are many external and internal limits to our capacity for reason. At the same time, our reason may monitor and critique our success at pursuing its own ideal use. It's important to keep in mind that rational thinking is not our only form of intelligence or source of knowledge. It is a very powerful tool, but it should be complemented by other spheres of intelligence such as emotional, aesthetic, and spiritual intelligence. Each one has its own domain and its own appropriate use. Our aesthetic intelligence will not necessarily help us in constructing logical arguments, but neither will our rational intelligence or linear thinking help us in the realm of the aesthetic. Our contemporary society tends to favor rational intelligence above all the other forms of intelligence, but they all have their appropriate and important spheres in which they reign. They can be misused too, not only by employing one form of intelligence in an unsuitable area, but even within their own sphere. For example, we can use "reason" to rationalize conclusions we want to reach, rather than to examine the reasoning dispassionately.

Fundamentalists tend to abuse rationality because they know which conclusions are acceptable and which are not. Furthermore, many "non-fundamentalists" are merely fundamentalist in less sweeping ways. They have their areas that resist unprejudiced inquiry. To a large extent, all of this falls under the category of the interpenetration of the emotional sphere with the rational sphere.

"The Truth Stands; a Lie Does Not Stand"

In the Babylonian Talmud (Tractate *Shabbat* 104a) we find the phrase *"kushta ka'ey, shikra la ka'ey"* (The truth stands; a lie does not stand), expressing the ideal of the unprejudiced pursuit of truth. Our vision of the truth is not static, however, and in certain ways we are always on a journey towards truth. What was believed to be true in the sixteenth century, for example, is not necessarily still seen as such today. That certainly applies to the sciences and many other fields as well. So how does this apply to revelation, religion, and the spiritual?

There are a few classic ways in which revelation is described in various traditions. One way claims that at some point in history a particular person (or in the case of the revelation at Sinai, an entire people) was graced with revelation and that people must accept and conform to the specifics of that revelation. A variation of this version accepts the revelation in general, but does not see the particulars of the revelation as applicable for all time. One more view is that there exists a timeless Truth that an individual can attain, which amounts to a personal revelation or "enlightenment."

In the mystical streams of traditional Judaism, the various orientations are merged. But what if one's personal revelation conflicts with the canonical account of revelation? *Kushta ka'ey, shikra la ka'ey*. The tradition can be seen as sowing the seeds for its own evolution in the command, *"tzedek, tzedek tirdof"* ("Justice, justice you shall pursue"; Deuteronomy 16:20), for example. Given this commitment to justice, it is irresponsible to rationalize injustice in our tradition by claiming that what may look like injustice is not and must be beyond our comprehension.

If our commitment is to truth, we must not negate its gift by saying that the traditional revelation is beyond our capacity to understand and, therefore, impossible to critique. This does not mean that whatever we perceive is reality or that we can never fall victim to illusion, but there are criteria that help us determine the validity of our visions and the conclusions we draw from them. This is where we most need our rational faculties. Our ethical sensibilities must also be as acute as possible. The alternative is relinquishing the responsibilities of making decisions and judgments that are part and parcel of fully realizing ourselves as adults. Deciding we are incapable of judgments is a judgment also, but one that shirks the responsibilities inherent in adulthood.

What might have appeared to be just two or three thousand years ago or even a century ago, may no longer appear just to us now. Clearly, between the biblical era and the rabbinic era there were shifts in people's sense of justice. For example, a clear case is the concept of *"ayin takhat ayin"* (an eye for an eye), which is interpreted in the Talmud (Tractate *Baba Kama* 84) to refer to monetary compensation for the injury.[1] Our sages examine the issue carefully and conclude that it only makes sense that the verse in Exodus must refer to monetary compensation and not an actual eye for an eye. But if that were the case, wouldn't it have been so much easier to write that in the first place and not require the elaborate argumentation to draw the monetary conclusion rather than the literal one? Why risk such a likelihood of people drawing a literal conclusion? The Talmudic discussion illustrates the sensibilities of the sages by their discomfort with a literal reading of *"ayin takhat ayin."*

Hopefully we are always on the path to the Promised Land where we live with the consciousness of, and consistently with, revelation, for we inevitably are engaged in an exodus from, or enslavement to, idolatry, however subtle the forces may be.

---

1. The Orthodox explain this problem away by asserting that the written Torah and the oral Torah (the Talmud) were both given at Sinai and therefore the teaching in *Baba Kama* is not much later , but actually contemporary with the passage in Exodus and meant to explain what the Torah truly intended in its own time.

Chapter 3

Avodah Zarah and Avodat Hashem

THE POTENTIAL FOR *AVODAH zarah*, or idol worship, exists whenever we confuse our means with our aims or become more committed to inherited beliefs than to a pursuit of wisdom and truth.
This is a much broader use of the term than is conventional. On
the opposite end of the spectrum is *avodat Hashem*, the worship
of or devotion to the Divine, to that which is ultimate. Elements of
both may coexist in anyone at any time. It is like the biblical passage Genesis 25:23 in which God informs Rebecca, *"shnei goyim
b'vitnekh"* (there are two nations in your womb), that is, two powers contending with each other.

Few, if any, of us think that the object of our devotion is an
idol yet choose to worship it anyway. *Avodah zarah* manifests in
many ways: from crass devotion to superficiality, to passive indif-
ference to plumbing the depths of Being, or far more subtle forms
in between. The way we respond to our own limitations should be
different from our response to others' limitations, but both cases
deserve compassion. The first-century BCE Talmudic sage Hillel
said, "Do not judge another until you are in his [or her] place"
(*Pirkei Avot* 2:5). But when are we ever truly in anyone else's place?

Most religious traditions invest an enormous amount of value in accepting prescribed beliefs. In some cases people have been
severely punished for questioning or rejecting those beliefs, even
to the point of death. This enormous investment in the acceptance

of prescribed beliefs can amount to a form of idolatry. This is particularly true when a person's intellectual faculties are considered more dangerous than beneficial. That surrounds the prescribed beliefs with a mystification that tries to place them beyond the powers of our mind. The irony is that sometimes people try to logically convince others to abandon trust in their own minds. In other words, they try to reason someone out of using their reason.

Some beliefs require nothing of their believers but a superficial assumption of truth. Others require an inner conviction that generally spills over into a person's behavior. Still others, such as religious beliefs, usually demand specific action.

Traditional Judaism is filled with these last expectations. What will maintain a person's commitment to behavior that hinges on a belief that cannot be proven? Generally it requires a love of the belief and/or a fear of the consequences of not conforming to it. To keep people obedient and toeing the line, either questioning must be diminished or fear must be amplified. Fundamentalism works on both fronts.

Nothing rivals an experience of the Presence of God. When that peak of what feels like eternity in the moment ends, hopefully its residue remains and changes the way we see everything. It's like God, which is in everything, has shown Its Face, has peeked out, has dazzled us, overwhelmed us with Its Presence, has made everything come alive in a way that is unimaginable. And when that experience recedes we may be in exile from paradise again, but the memory of having touched the soil and breathed the air of that Promised Land may sustain us.

There is a traditional attitude that each successive generation since the revelation at Sinai grows weaker in its connection to and understanding of Torah. In other words, the farther we are from a personal experience of the Divine Presence, the more tenuous our commitment to it and the more it relies on faith, which is less compelling than experience. The farther we are from experience, the more susceptible we are to *avodah zarah*, to idol worship. Something that is "*zar*" ("*zarah*" is the feminine inflection) is outside ourselves; it is "foreign," strange. The most immediate devotion is one generated from inside, that is, from our own experience. The farther we get from that, the more our beliefs and devotion can stray "outside."

If we define idolatry too broadly, we dilute its significance. The Torah clearly sees a world abounding in abominations and zealously condemns them. But if we cease to give credence to the image of an irritable deity condemning idol worship and threatening those who engage in it, what significance does idolatry retain for us? People don't consciously choose idolatry over a deeper vision of God. It is parallel to the revelation/exodus example, in which every new level of understanding brings us to the realization that until now we too were unwittingly idolatrous.

We are born with inherent limitations and inherent potentialities, and an unavoidable ignorance as to the parameters of either. No diagnostic test can reveal what is truly within us. We can honor the gift of life by trying to be as fully human as possible and by nourishing our and other people's potentials. As the Hasidic tale about Reb Zusya says, when the time would come at the end of his life to make an accounting of his soul, Zusya was not worried that the Master of the Universe would ask, "Zusya, why were you not Moses?" but rather, "Why were you not Zusya?" This Zusya story assumes some degree of free will in directing our lives. We may be servants to our proclivities and habits, but we do have the capacity for choice and change. We may be constitutionally built to respond to certain stimuli, but within the range of possible responses we have the potential for choice. External, behavioral change may be easier than inner change, but both are possible.

People are not born equally configured intellectually, physically, or emotionally. Those inequities mean that not all people have the same possibilities. The variable, the wild card, is our ability to choose and to change. We can change our physical, intellectual, and emotional environments and affect our activities and inner growth.

The Trajectory of One's Life

We can view the trajectory of a person's life from various perspectives. Among the possibilities is the development and nurturing of one's own soul and the nurturing of others. The tradition puts it as *"kol yisrael arevim zeh ba'zeh"* (all Jews are responsible for each other; Babylonian Talmud, Tractate *Shevuot* 39a). The more we nurture our inner life within the context of the community, the more we may affect, to some degree, the lives of those we encounter. The more the consciousness and adhesiveness of the community evolves, the more it has the ability to positively affect its individual members. If you encounter people in your synagogue community, for example, really praying or studying or chanting seriously, that has some effect. If the community goes on a retreat together, that can also create a greater bond between members, but can also affect the development of individuals. People being in classes together to develop some spiritual tools like meditation, prayer, Hebrew language, etc. all can have an effect on other people within the group.

The first of the Ten Commandments, *"Anokhi YHVH Elohekha"* (I am YHVH your God), the *mitzvah* to recognize the Eternal One, contains within it all the others. The first word in it, that is, *"anokhi"* ("I" or "I am"—since Hebrew lacks the verb "to be" in the present tense), and ultimately even the first letter of it, the ineffable *aleph*, contains them all. If one truly glimpses the Infinite Presence that is *anokhi*, how can one act idolatrously? The same is true if one is able to experience the *niggun*, the melody/vibration, of the ineffable *aleph*. We have a tendency to understand silence as a lack of sound, whereas in this case it's more accurate to understand it as a fullness that only no sound can express. The command of *"anokhi"* is the challenge to experience it more fully, just as the challenge of any moment in our lives is to more consciously live that moment. This is the lifelong task of increasing awareness, of investing each moment with a more palpable sense of the Presence of the Eternal or, more realistically, increasing the level and frequency of these moments.

During the vicissitudes of a lifetime, this process undergoes peaks and valleys. The recollection of a peak experience can spare us from investing too much in visions seen while dwelling in the valleys, or in any of the territory in between. Idolatry confounds the landscape of *"Mitzrayim"* with the Promised Land. When we forget that we are always in one *Mitzrayim* or another on our way to the Promised Land and confuse the two, we begin to treat the moment idolatrously.

"Torah" and/or "the Torah"

To a person who believes in an anthropomorphic deity behind the events in history, the views expressed in this book will appear idolatrous and certainly heretical. To someone who identifies with the orientation expressed in these pages, however, a belief in an anthropomorphic deity is quite idolatrous. A prevalent understanding of God in one era may, in a later stage of Jewish history, become tantamount to idolatry. In the past, this type of declaration would be avoided by reading the new perspective into the more ancient one. Not being able to adopt that posture in all good conscience does not diminish the Torah as the founding document of the tradition, but does render its authority less absolute.

When the Midrash *(Bereshit Rabbah I)* says that God looked into the Torah to create the universe, and later Kabbalistic literature states that *"kudsha brikh hu v'oraita khad hu"* (The Blessed Holy One and Torah are One), they have elevated Torah to a status beyond that implied here. If we accept these formulas, however, as an inspired depiction of *torah elyonah*, sublime Torah, or *"p'nimiyut hatorah,"* the deepest recesses or "soul" of the Torah, then this Torah, as ultimate Teaching rather than physical document captured in ink on parchment, would fit our sense of Torah as perennial process unfolding into the world and into consciousness. This is also the difference between speaking of "Torah" (as in, "Moses received Torah at Sinai"; *Pirkei Avot* 1:1) and *"hatorah"* (the Torah).

Torah without the definite article is open-ended and consistent with the sense of process inherent in all teaching. "*The* Torah," by dint of being a sealed document, is less so.[1] We can glean new "Torah" from the Torah, and have a long history of doing so in the guise of uncovering the deeper contents of canonized words. The distinction here is not merely semantic. Drawing wisdom and inspiration from words of the Torah because they articulate or point towards great truths without pledging absolute allegiance to every explicit or implicit doctrine articulated in Scripture combines a reverence for Torah with receptivity to evolving insights. Otherwise we become locked in to accepting and/or justifying attitudes that can offend a person more sensitized to certain issue such as, for example, the Torah's attitudes towards women, homosexuality, and non-believers or ambivalent believers.

In the Torah itself there are what appear to be different Divine voices and stances. We encounter a volatile God while we also find the sublime Voice of "*Ehyeh asher Ehyeh*" (I shall be what I shall be). It is the "*Ehyeh*" voice that compels Moses to go back and redeem the people from *Mitzrayim*. In this image, the intra-human and Divine-human encounters merge. Moses encounters God via the "humble" bush and stands in intimate relation with the Eternal. This state naturally demands compassionate, loving engagement between humans. The *Ehyeh* voice, the voice of endless Becoming, the sense of the increasingly palpable Divine in this world, demands ethical behavior. It compels us to relate to the divinity, the soul, of each thing. So Moses must reenter the world of *Mitzrayim*, of narrowness, and bring the people redemption, not simply horde his Divine encounters for himself.

Who/What Is "Adam"?

In many ways Moses embodies the mortal ideal implied in the root of the word for "human being" in Hebrew, *adam (aleph, dalet,*

---

1. *Khazal* (our sages of blessed memory) already in *Pirkei Avot* 5:22 saw the depths of the Torah as endless: "*hafokh bah v'hafokh bah d'khola bah*" (turn her—that is, the Torah—and turn her, for everything is in her).

mem). In Genesis 2:7 it is written that YHVH *Elohim* created *adam* dust from the *adamah,* the earth, and blew into *adam, nishmat khayyim,* the breath (or soul) of life. One component of *adam* is related to *adamah,* earth, the solidly physical. This is also related to *dam,* blood. I would like to add one more key for understanding *adam:* the word *dom,* silence.

Maimonides, following Aristotle, characterized humans as the highest level of earthly existence: *"m'daber,"* speaker. But *dom,* silence, is another crucial pillar of the essence of *adam.* The speaking one and the embodied one are both characterized by "doing," but *dom,* being silent, is a gateway to purely "being," a state that facilitates full presence, a state with which we seek to anchor our lives via meditation. When we are in a fully receptive, porous state of *dom* we may unite with the ineffable *"aleph"* that is part of being *adam* (spelled *aleph, dalet, mem).* Finally, *aleph* is the initial letter of every first-person singular future-tense verb, that is, the "I will . . ." component of every verb.

Every aspect of *adam* is realized fully in the being of Moses. Moses, according to the tradition, not only has the deepest connection to Divinity, but also is the greatest leader of the community. His guiding of the community, which is his most "embodied" work, is an outgrowth of his vision of God and his ability to be in the Divine Presence. One other quality characterizing Moses in the Torah and tradition is humility. He is *"ish anav"* (Numbers 12:3), the humble one. This humility is intimately linked to his relationship with God, being the only one to truly experience the Divine *"panim el panim,"* "face to face" or rather "depth to depth"(since the same root—*peh, nun, mem*—also means "inside" or "within"). In the Kabbalistic tradition, Moses is the only one who sees the Eternal through *"aspeklaria m'irah"* (a shining, transparent speculum).

The more intimate the encounter with the Eternal, the more humbling the experience. This is called *"bittul hayesh,"* which is often depicted as an overriding or transcending of one's ego and one's "subjective" thoughts. True *bittul hayesh,* however, comes from being overwhelmed by the Divine Presence to the point of losing the perspective of distance and separation. The individual consciousness becomes subsumed in the greater constellation of unity. The fingernail is identifiable as a separate entity, as is the brain cell, but they are also part of the one body. Both are simultaneously true. *Bittul hayesh* is descriptive of moments so absorbed in the consciousness of unity that awareness of the simultaneous reality of separateness is lost.

Bittul hayesh doesn't come from flogging one's ego into submission. One's ego, when healthy, enhances life, that very life which is permeated by the Divine. Having a sense of oneself enables one to *daven* (to "pray"), to occupy oneself with Torah, to feel potent enough to affect some *tikkun olam* (repair of the world). It is an offense to the sanctity of creation, I think, to dismiss it as null or illusory. At the same time, it is idolatrous to elevate it to an ultimate status, a status only appropriate to the Eternal. Each life is of immeasurable value, but we need to keep the perspective of both the sacredness of each element of creation and the ultimate reverence due the One.

Different perspectives on reality can be simultaneously valid. Returning to the analogy of the brain cell or fingernail as part of the unity of the entire body, each component's viewpoint is valid, though the perspective of the entire entity is more complete. The entire "organism" functions at its best when all its parts function well in their roles. When one component ceases to function in harmony with other parts, disease occurs. The ego has its healthy function: it is only problematic when it is inflated and tries to function outside its appropriate domain.

Between Monism and Dualism

A sense of self can be a starting point of prayer. At the same time, we may be granted the grace of experiencing the Divinity of our essence. This is very different from confusing ourselves with God. Every cell is part of the entire body, but not identical with it. Ideally, through prayer we can deepen our awareness of, and connection to, the All-Pervasive and All-Encompassing One. Experiencing in some manner this Presence is an overwhelmingly humbling experience as well as often a powerfully exhilarating one. To say that we are all part of the One and yet that One also vastly transcends all that we are is to say that some combination of monism and dualism operates simultaneously.

Not recognizing the humility appropriate to our place in the cosmos is comparable to seeing one person or group of people as inherently more cosmically or spiritually significant than others. Both exhibit arrogance. Certainly many cultures have spawned cosmologies beginning from where they stood and subsequently saw that place as the center. A democratic vista recognizes that many peoples may see themselves as standing at the center of the universe, and, from a relative perspective, they are. Confusing a relative perspective with an absolute one is what characterizes its arrogance.

So how different is that process from the dynamic of giving full credence to the conclusions of our own reasoning? Is that also arrogant bordering on idolatrous? Are we inflating the value and validity of our reason? What are the alternatives? Whether we give ourselves up to a belief in "revealed" religion of a more or less fundamentalist stripe or we pledge allegiance to the world of reason, or the senses, or any other creed, we ultimately make that choice by some act of reasoning, however rigorous or lax. The most we can strive for is to do so in good faith, meaning that we don't draft our rational faculties to the service of rationalizing our foregone faith conclusions. As in Plato's analogy of confusing shadows on the cave walls with the entities casting those shadows, we can recognize that our rational faculties are limited, but so are all our other faculties, whether our senses, our imagination, or our "intuition," etc. All of those faculties together are the tools by which we navigate our journey in this world. If we make a conscious choice to denigrate and/or neglect some faculties, we do so in good faith. It is disingenuous, however, to employ our reason to negate the validity of reason. If it is invalid, how can we trust the conclusions to which it leads us? We can recognize its limitations, but recognizing them, obviously, does not imply the truth of any non-reasoned assertion.

The Idolatry of Faith

A common flaw of fundamentalism is the failure by many to recognize that faith is not always a choice. Some people come to it naturally and others do not. Some people may make a choice to try to believe and in fact they may opt to ignore their critical and rational faculties. Fundamentalism often elevates faith to a totally inappropriate status, such as making "truth" claims regarding the object of faith. Making a submission to faith a major value and subsequently judging others by their acceptance of the contents of the particular faith seems ludicrous, but no more so than expecting people to reject other parts of themselves. When I was in college a new band was formed called Blind Faith (with Eric Clapton, Ginger Baker, and Stevie Winwood). When my roommate asked me by way of making a pun in an approving way if I had "blind faith," I responded, "Absolutely not!"

How can you fault another person for lacking faith? Faith is not something you can will. Can someone in good conscience ignore his or her thoughts? Doing so would be tantamount to demanding that the other person excise their critical and rational faculties. Once you begin demanding the constriction of any part of a person's makeup, whether rational, emotional, physical, psychological, or spiritual, you begin to create a distorted person.

It requires radical surgery to conform this view to some of the sublime insights of the mystical tradition, which speak of *Ayn Sof*, the Infinite One beyond all description, and of *devekut*, uniting, with the Divine. Theoretically, one could speak of "becoming one" with a sort of dwarfed deity, too. The goal and concept of *devekut*, of uniting and merging with the Divine, doesn't preclude very limited understandings of what God is. However limited and constricted the comprehension of God, one could still long to merge with that deity. However, the meaning of "uniting" with God has a significantly different sense when the understanding of God is so different. So what is the relationship between that concept and any "knowable" reality "out there"?

The experience of *devekut* is a subjective one and doesn't preclude an idolatrous relationship with some "false" deity. A person's ethical life could be very sensitized and cultivated while their spiritual or aesthetic sensibilities remain relatively dull. But what difference does this attempt at objective verification make? As is the case with an aesthetic experience, a spiritual experience of encounter with the Eternal One is deeply private. We are alone with our God, though we may live in a community of fellow travelers similarly alone. This neither proves nor denies the "reality" of the experience. There is no "ultimate" external arbiter of the greatness or depth of a work of art. There are no objective measurements for Divine encounters.

Can we measure love or any other internal, non-physical experience? We might be able to gauge external responses that seem to be evoked by the internal experience, but all we know about the internal experience is what the "subject" reports. So here is another scenario in which the roles of different faculties complement each other.

Rationality and Spirituality

Spiritual intelligence and rational intelligence can nurture each other. Whereas a spiritual sensibility vivifies life and brings the taste of the Eternal into the arena of the immediate, rational intelligence reflects upon the experience and endeavors to grasp and assimilate it, examining how the experience informs our comprehension of the world and what demands it makes of us. Each faculty has its appropriate sphere. Reason, for all its power, is not necessarily the right category or quality of thought required to grasp spiritual truths. Non-rational intelligence and insights are generally more relevant. However, the rational mind can critique them, inspecting for irrationality. Beliefs, at best, are only partially arrived at by reason. Experience, and hopefully examined experience, is more important. Though experience itself is not rational per se, the degree of credibility we lend our experiences should be tempered by reason.

One person's idol is another's "absolute truth." The ability to imagine an increasingly encompassing "concept" of God doesn't necessitate a reality behind the exercise of imagination. Nor does it preclude one. And here we return to our understanding of *adam*. Though imagination is a powerful tool, it can at best lead us to the threshold that only experience can cross. *Dom*, the *kol d'mamah dakah*, the subtle sound of silence, is a state of being we must experience, not imagine. It is not a concept. Rather, the experience of it may engender concepts that we struggle to articulate for others, striving to explain where we have been, not what we have imagined.

The experience of the All-Encompassing, All-Pervasive One defies definition. Defining something is a rational category of thought and an inadequate one for the experience of the sublime. Language such as poetry may attempt to communicate an experience that overwhelms one's consciousness, but poetry often uses non-rational forms of language for that very reason, in an attempt to capture something that conventional language can't approach.

People have devoted a lot of energy to philosophical speculation about God. The experience of what feels like infinite transcendence and eternal immediacy overlaps with some philosophical categories applied to God, but isn't confined to them. As has often been said, the god of the "philosophers" doesn't evoke the passion of devotion.

Devotion, however, can often be triggered by very anthropomorphic views of the Divine. These views of God can evoke psychologically and emotionally sweeping dedication, just like a domineering parent or monarch might evoke. Devotion in itself, obviously, is no guarantee of a sound spirituality. Devotion may vitalize some aspects of a person's being, but inhibit others. For example, it might inhibit a person's psychological and emotional growth by transplanting adolescent or even childlike dynamics onto the spiritual realm. It may require a submission of our rationality to the demands of a tyrannical (even if benevolent) deity. When our faculties function harmoniously with each other, we can grow and mature as a total person. Idolatry stifles this kind of growth, particularly when it suppresses part of the person into submission to its limited understanding of God. An idolatrous society is a punishing environment.

Materialism, Sensuality, and Spirituality

The dominant orientation in Western society today is deeply materialistic. Even those elements of society that are generally the reserve of the spiritual tend towards a fairly shallow sense of it. Much of religion confuses the spiritual with that which is not quite material but is far from a sense of the All-Encompassing, All-Pervasive Presence that I've been referring to in these pages. So much energy is invested in acquisition and in creating commodities out of all aspects of our lives. Even religion is "sold" to the public. (It often feels it has to "compete" in the marketplace of ideas). The life of the senses is the main attraction, seducing people into a lifestyle of acquisition.

The senses can bring us deep intimacy, connection, and vast comprehension. At the same time, they can lead us on a path that remains forever superficial. Connection to the soul of anything or anyone is not commodifiable, exchangeable, or disposable. It is the antithesis of all these qualities. Since these qualities are the staples of a consumer society, a focus on depth, on the eternal rather than the ephemeral, is out of sync with the dominant materialist orientation.

Why are we so easily seduced? The surface is generally the first part of ourselves to experience anything and the first aspect of anything that we experience. If we fail to register that so much richness resides below the surface, we will constantly seek the momentary titillation of the surface. Depth generally requires effort—not only the effort to continually cultivate what is subtle and, therefore, elusive, but also the effort to not settle into the more immediate gratification offered by the less sublime. "*Avodah*" ("worship" or "work") is the apt word, for devotion or worship requires an effort. Little of value is attainable or sustainable without devotion. We may develop habits of devotion, which is akin to

maintaining the fitness and flexibility that habitual exercise promotes. Idolatry appeals to the part of us that longs to stay at rest,
that wants the security of easy answers and is willing to ignore their
fallacious underpinnings because it's less demanding. The sense of
endless Becoming can feel destabilizing, as when something that
seemed certain one day suddenly no longer is. This doesn't imply
that nothing survives the process of perpetual Becoming, the dy-
namism of *Ehyeh* ("I will be"). The existence of a tradition testifies
to continuity in the midst of perpetual change.

If our tradition becomes sealed off from critical thought or
becomes more important than a living connection with God, then
it too becomes an idol stifling essential elements of our humanity
in order to survive. The tradition's existence, though, is meaningful
beyond its utilitarian aspects. It is a repository of visceral wisdom
in addition to being a path to sanctifying our lives. On the other
hand, when it impedes our seeing the world and the Divine more
clearly, we can appreciate the role it once filled without feeling we
must preserve it intact at the expense of our souls. Its instinct for
self-preservation is often so strong, though, that it stigmatizes as
heretical those who reject it. However, sometimes the heretics of
one generation prove to be the prophets of the next.

Though all times are transitional, as mentioned above, the
rate of change has greatly accelerated. Change is not synonymous
with progress or improvement necessarily. We need to examine
specific changes and gauge their impact and relevance to our spiritual lives. The growing sophistication of technology has greatly
facilitated our ability to communicate and gather information and
to scientifically probe the universe with sharper precision, but
it hasn't altered the most fundamental facts of our lives—birth,
death, and the craving for meaning.

Technology is a powerful tool and, like any tool, it can be
used for growth and in ways that promote a meaningful life or it
can be used destructively and in ways that distract and foster superficiality. Technology such as computers or television can spread
information and raise the general educational level of society, or
it can spread misinformation and depress the educational level of

society with more distractions from the questions and issues that touch upon the very meaning of our lives and even leave us more susceptible to those who would manipulate us for their own material gain and our general detriment. "I consume, therefore I am" is not a very profound approach to life. It supports the economic structure of societies and derails the addressing of more timeless issues. These timeless issues persist in the form of evolving answers to perennial questions. The sense and the experience of the Eternal endures, though how we comprehend it is modified in relationship to how we understand existence in general.

Embodying Spirituality

Historically, giving physical expression to the Divine has been anathema to Judaism, and it wasn't uncommon for those zealous for the life of the spirit to disparage the physical altogether and to even see it as a root of evil. Such a position negates the experience of the Divine as *m'malei kol almin*, the Immanent God filling all creation. What can be the meaning of the phrase "God's *kavod* [literally, "glory"] fills the entire earth" (Isaiah 6:3) when we belittle the very physical life of the body that defines us, that is, the part of *adam* that is *adamah* (earth) and *dam* (blood)? Such an orientation avoids engaging in the struggle to sanctify the daily life inevitably lived by most people, as though we need to negate the very humanity that defines us in order to live sanctified lives.

All primal forces have the potential to be sanctified or desecrated. Sidestepping the struggle is avoiding the possibility of being more grandly human and more spiritually realized through refining these aspects of our lives. Removing oneself from life in the body or life in society fosters the illusion that one has transcended challenging aspects of human life, whereas in fact one has merely eliminated the possibility of sanctifying those very arenas of life. One's spirituality may appear more pronounced, but it's a distorted perspective because various elements that would throw things into relief have been eliminated from view. This is not meant to criticize those who pursue this path, but rather to emphasize that it is not *the* path, but *a* path, and one with serious weaknesses for the very goals it espouses. It curtails the fullness of human life and consequently the areas in which the spiritual may flourish. Rather than bringing holiness and the Divine Presence into more areas of human experience, it greatly restricts the realms touched by sanctity. Plus it ignores the reality of most people's lives.

Rather than reject our physicality, the part of us that is *adamah* and *dam*, it is desirable to experience the *dom* (silence) that presides and vivifies it perpetually. Better that we truly learn to hear, as the *Sh'ma* suggests, not the static of the superficial, but rather the *kol d'mamah dakah*, the subtle sound of silence of the One.

In Proverbs 3:6 it says, *"b'khol d'rakhekha da'ehu"* ("In all your ways [or paths] know 'Him/It,'" that is, God). This can be understood as the mystics understood it: that we should know (that is, be intimately merged with) God in everything we do. This expresses a fully embodied spirituality. God fills all creation and can be found in every aspect of it. This requires no proof text. We don't need a proof text to confirm that what we experience is what we experience. We don't need a proof text to confirm that nature is wondrous and pulsing with the Divine. We need a proof text only to confirm that our ancestors shared this perception. This is why Walt Whitman could write in "Song of Myself" (canto 24), "Divine am I inside and out . . . / This head more than churches, bibles, and all the creeds." Although he was neither a traditionalist nor a biblical scholar, Whitman had a powerful sense of the sanctity of all life and of the Divine as *m'malei kol almin*, filling all universes. Furthermore, he saw how far the organized religions known to him had drifted from this sensibility. This remains true in our own days as well.

Avodah Zarah, idolatry, always stifles some major aspect of our humanity, retaining intact a dwarfed deity, in this instance a deity too sterile or finicky for the real world that God pervades! But the biblical phrase *"b'khol d'rakhekha da'ehu"* urges a fully human expression of *avodat Hashem*, devotion to the spiritual depths of Life, in its glorious fullness.

Chapter 4

Kavana and Meditative Prayer

SPIRITUAL AND RELIGIOUS CLAIMS are not verifiable in the way that logical or scientific statements are. They have their own internal logic and consistency, which becomes clearer once you are familiar with the terrain. The visceral aspects of our lives are the stuff of poetry, the immeasurable dimensions of experience that only the Heart of Wisdom comprehends. Our use of the word "know" as in "knowing God" or as in "Adam knew Eve" is not the sort of experience that can be measured or tested. It is subjective, as all emotions are subjective or as any aesthetic experience is subjective, but that does not diminish its vital role and meaning.

What makes one performance of a piece of music, for example, more alive or transporting than another is not only the technical ability of the performer, but the heart, the soul, and the life that the performer invests in it. The Hebrew term for such an infusion of oneself into an act or experience is "*kavana.*" *Kavana* is an intangible quality, though one that is utterly real and meaningful to the person who can bring the core of him/herself into activities and consciousness.

Though the abstractness of the term "core" makes its definition slippery, it doesn't diminish its meaningfulness. To define is to limit, which is appropriate to linear thought more than to non-linear thought. We may be able to define the term "music," for example, but what makes music powerful, beautiful, and moving is not its linear, verifiable qualities, but rather the lived experience of it, which is more elusive of definition. Terms applicable to the realm of the spiritual are words in this latter category.

Terms like "*kavana*" and "soul" speak meaningfully to those who experience them, but remain almost inexplicable to those who do not. This is comparable to attempting to communicate an exquisite sensation or taste to someone who has never felt that sensation or experienced a similar taste: the more unique the taste or experience, the greater the difficulty in describing it. However, when two people who are familiar with this kind of experience communicate, there can be a mutual understanding despite the privacy of the experience. Familiarity with this quality of experience is the essential element. This is one of the meanings of the traditional term "*hamayvin yavin*" (the person of understanding will understand).

Though it embodies several meanings, the term *kavana*, broadly speaking, is the process of entering into an activity or state as fully as possible, that is, attempting to put as much of one's consciousness into that act or state. To cultivate *kavana* is to learn to focus consciousness.

Consciousness and attention are not synonymous. Paying attention allows consciousness to enter, but it does not guarantee its quality. Analogously, you can stand in front of a painting and be very attentive to it, but that cannot ensure you a high-quality of experience. The quality of the experience is determined by the being or entity we encounter and the level of consciousness we bring to the encounter.

The more we are able to experience the All-Pervasive One, the more we encounter it in the "other," regardless of how transparent or relatively opaque it may be in the "other." Nature often provides an easier access to the All-Pervasive One, because of both its beauty and the life force so tangible in it. The more palpable the life force, the more easily you can recognize Presence, but our ability is dependent on the consciousness we've cultivated and nurtured. We can read this in Jacob's epiphany in Genesis 28, where he says, "Indeed YHVH is in this *makom* [place] and *Anokhi lo yadati* [literally, 'I didn't know']."

"*Anokhi*" ("I" or "I am") is not only the first word of the Ten Commandments, but the first "commandment" itself. In other words, the first of the Ten Commandments is the recognition of God's Presence. "*Anokhi*," the Divine Presence, the *m'malei kol al-min*, the All-Pervasive One, was in that place and moment, which is every place and moment. We are always in that place and that moment until we experience Presence where we are. This is the spiritual vision we all potentially possess. This is a way of reading the morning blessing "*pokeakh ivrim*," that the Divine "opens the eyes of the blind"; that is, until we see the spiritual dimension of the All-Pervasive Divinity, we are "blind" in that realm of vision. That experience is a question of consciousness. So Jacob can be understood as saying he didn't "know" "*Anokhi*." The immanent Presence of Divinity that "indeed is in this place" was previously opaque to him.

Kavana and Cultivating Consciousness

How is consciousness cultivated? How do we learn to look or listen deeply? A necessary step is learning to pay attention and focus on whatever we are encountering rather than focusing on the "I" who believes s/he is doing the encountering. *Kavana*, or that intention and direction of one's awareness and investment of one's being in the experience, helps to keep the "I" out of the way, facilitating the opening of consciousness. This is comparable to the levels and qualities of silence that we can experience. A shallow silence is a mere absence of sound. A deeper silence is a resonant silence, a silence that is not "dead," but vibrantly alive. We too often hear without listening and look without seeing. In each of these realms, there are many levels of being present and attuned.

There is no escape from the many meanings of certain terms. *Kavana* can be understood in a way in which the "I" is very conscious of itself. This type of *kavana*—which generally seeks to preserve the sense of oneself as separate from the "object" of *kavana*—has its place, its strengths, and its weaknesses, which are relevant or not depending on the circumstances. For our purposes, when speaking in relation to acts *beyn adam lamakom* (between ourselves and the Omnipresent), that sense of *kavana* which fosters separateness interferes with an awareness of the All-Pervasive, All-Encompassing One. My intent is not to denigrate those who desire to cultivate a sense of separateness, but to recognize that it is more consistent with an anthropomorphic sense of God (even one that is camouflaged in less anthropomorphic language).

Those who feel awed by the power of God conceived of as "other," that is, as exclusively outside ourselves, may understand God as the All-Encompassing One, but they usually conceive of God as some distant Will that resides beyond the realm of creation. This is not a semantic trifle, but a fundamental difference that seriously influences how we perceive creation. Such a view of God as a distant Will may evoke awe and fear because this Will generally implies a judgment that goes along with it and, consequently, reward and punishment, thus emerging more clearly as an anthropomorphic deity. A grasp of God as Ultimate Being and Becoming is analogous to experiencing the ocean as an overwhelming power and presence, the activity of which is part of its essence, not a result of some premeditated will. The waves of the ocean are part of its nature, not a product of its will. God *is*, and everything is part of God's Being.[1]

Attuning to that Presence is an overwhelming experience. It is not one that makes us cower for the consequences of our lapses in ritual or long for the desserts of our fulfilled "*mitzvot*," as though some ultimate judge will reward or punish us. Rather, it is an experience that awes us into wanting to stay in harmony with that life force because all else seems to miss the most fundamental point. As it says in *Pirkei Avot* 4:1, "the reward of a *mitzvah* is a *mitzvah*, the 'reward' [or 'consequence'] of a transgression is transgression." The act itself is its own reward or punishment. If it is in harmony with Being, that is, with God, this is a clear reward. If not, that lack

1. Here the word "Being" is not meant as an entity alone, but as a combination of Entity and State, that is, as both noun and verb simultaneously—what both the Kabbalists and Maimonides would describe as the Knowing, the Knower, and the Known simultaneously.

of harmony is its own punishment. The greater the consciousness and experience of harmony via an act, the greater the "reward."

Prayer as Its Own Reward

Each word of prayer is also its own reward or punishment. Is it in harmony with Divinity and does it foster harmony with all Being, or does it foster distance or alienation from the Divine? The attempt to be *"nikhnas,"* "to enter into" an act or word (as opposed to the goal of being *"yotzei,"* "fulfilling the traditional obligation"), enhances receptivity to experiencing the Presence in an act or word. The less attention we pay to our part in saying or doing things, the more we may become *"nikhnas"* and thus receptive to the life force harbored in that act or word. Being receptive doesn't guarantee an experience, but rather facilitates it. Again, divesting ourselves of the "I" is a byproduct of entering the act or word, not vice versa. In other words, we don't achieve a state of *"nikhnas"* by focusing on distancing ourselves from the "I" who's acting or speaking. Such attempts generally achieve the opposite of their intended goals.

Understanding each utterance as its own reward is central to comprehending *kavana* in terms of prayer. *Kavana,* as it is being used here, is essentially the ability to be *"nikhnas"* vis-à-vis any act or utterance. There are innumerable degrees of this, but grading oneself is antithetical to the entire enterprise. The intention of being *"nikhnas"* is ultimately to taste and experience *devekut,* union, to transcend distance and separation, to know the Divinity that pervades and transcends all.[2]

In the realm of prayer, trying to be *"yotzei,"* that is, fulfilling the (traditional) obligation to pray, is consistent with a perspective of judgment and commandment as a function of an external, distant divine Will, not of Will as synonymous with God's Being (as in the analogy of the relationship of waves to the ocean). The *"yotzei"*

2. It should be noted that *"devekut"* is traditionally understood in various ways. See Moshe Idel's *Kabbalah: New Perspectives,* 35–58 (New Haven: Yale University Press, 1988). The connotation used in these pages is one implying "union" with the Divine.

orientation towards prayer is consistent with petitionary prayer and thus naturally raises the question of prayers being answered or not, which is an anthropomorphic type of question regarding our relationship with God. The orientation of being "*nikhnas*" is quite different, perceiving all prayer as its own reward. Petitionary and propitiatory prayer seems utterly beside the point. Whether you floated or swam in the "ocean" is the concern, not whether you turned the course of the tide to fit your request. What words of prayer will facilitate this experience? Words of praise that are consistent with the consciousness of God as all-pervasive and all-encompassing, not as judging, rewarding, and punishing.

Words of praise in prayer can also be expressed, however, from the perspective of distance and separation, with a desire to sustain those qualities. The craving for closeness can also exist towards a deity seen as a parent or monarch. A child yearns to be close to his or her parent; a subject seeks to draw close to the king. Words of praise can feel very appropriate to people with these perspectives. In fact, the very same words of praise may apply. What differentiates the identical words in such different cases is the consciousness of the person using them and his/her *kavana*. "*Kavana*" here means "intention," coming from the root *(kaf, vav, nun)* meaning directing, direction, etc. In other words, *kavana* is what we "intend" when we say or do something and how we direct and focus our consciousness when saying or doing it.

The *kavana* and consciousness we bring to our use of words makes all the difference. If we intend the words as fully as we're capable of doing, we attempt to enter our words. The words become a vehicle and a bridge between the separate being who desires to pray and who, in doing so, may ultimately lose a sense of separateness by entering the words that reflect various aspects of Divinity.

Blessings

Let's take, as an example of *kavana*, the first words of any *b'rakha* (blessing), which are among the most significant words we'll ever pray. We begin any prayer with a sense of some distance, enough to be able to address God as "You." No matter how close we may feel, we still experience sufficient distance to use the word "*atah*" (You). We begin the *b'rakha* with the word "*barukh*" (blessed). The word "*barukh*" has enough elasticity to embody various meanings, but I'm concerned here with the meaning that most facilitates a state of being "*nikhnas*" and will render the prayer more "meditative." "*Barukh*" describes a state of being, a state of blessedness, imbued with Presence. This is how I understand the word "*barukh*" when addressed to God. One who says "*barukh*" and fully "means" this word (that is, experiences the meaning of the word) is in some way attempting to connect to that sense and state of blessedness that fills and surrounds us.

You cannot simply mouth the word and enter it fully. By merely mouthing it the word passes through us or "grazes" us, but makes little to no impression. To actually step into such a potent word is an immense task; to fully intend this word requires a consciousness of, and some connection to, the state of blessedness that God is. To utter the first word, "*barukh*," with the *kavana* the word itself invites is a lofty goal.

Though there remains a sense of distance in saying "*atah*" (You) in a *b'rakha*, the ability to feel ourselves "facing" the Divine, and not in an anthropomorphic way (which would deflate this word and address), is daunting. It requires an attempt to take these words of the *b'rakha* out of the conceptual realm so that we are not thinking about the words or even contemplating their meaning. Their meaning cannot be cornered and pinned down by the intellect. Our rational minds may lead us to the threshold we must cross over to begin to grasp these words and thus intend and ultimately live them as we "pray" them. Only with the fullness of our being can we possibly address the Divine to the point where we transcend our smaller self and enter the more transparently Divine level of our being, becoming ready to say the word "*Adonai*."

We are told in the Torah not to take God's Name in vain. We can understand this on a *pshat* (literal) level, or we can try and grasp it more subtly. We never pronounce the Name (since we lack the knowledge of its pronunciation), but substitute "*Adonai*" (literally, "my Lord") for it instead. Who could imagine ever pronouncing the Name without taking it in vain?

The closest we might come is the fullest silence, a silence that would blossom with the expansion of our consciousness and never reach an endpoint. Who would not be rendered "heavy of tongue" when overwhelmed by the Divine Presence? The unpronounceable nature of the Name itself is the ideal music to accompany its intention.

Protecting the Power of Words

Words have great power, and that power is nurtured and protected by our tending to them. If we overuse them, or use them with inadequate *kavana*, we drain their energy. For our language to retain or gain potency, we must cultivate it and not be promiscuous with it. But it would be a grave error to conclude that there's no room for humor in life if God is so central. An overbearing seriousness can squeeze the life out of language as much as an incessant frivolity can trivialize it. There is no formula for the ideal proportions of the two—precise formulas are symptomatic of a stiffness that suffocates language and most anything else it touches. Part of what can make great poetry is a playfulness and spontaneity with words. Poetry requires the "music" of the words—which is provided by the combination of sound, sense, rhythm, and timing—and the intelligence, insight, etc. that the words convey. Prayer is often a form of poetry attempting to capture an intensified speech that articulates depth. As with poetry there can be no immutable rules. Sometimes the most blunt, unembellished utterance captures the moment, and at other times words that are more intricate provide the needed vehicle.

Sometimes the strength and spirit of prayer is best attained spontaneously, while other times require the established prayers of the tradition. Sometimes prayer is not the optimal vehicle at all, but some action, silence, or meditation is. If we are going to fully inhabit our bodies and simultaneously cultivate our consciousness of the Divine, we need to sanctify the numerous aspects of our lives and not relegate the life of the spirit to some corner of our life or moment of our week. Though spiritual disciplines keep spiritual "muscles" toned, it is important to recognize that there may be countless methods and paths to this same end and the more we foster homogeneity, the more we tend to dehumanize the individual. The greater the variety of cultures, the more amplified our understanding of what it means to be human. The greater the wealth of flora and fauna on this planet, the greater our potential grasp of what life on this planet entails. The less we attempt to homogenize human spirituality and spiritual paths, the more we refine and broaden our comprehension of the entire enterprise.

A useful framework for navigating these areas is bearing in mind the dual concerns of *beyn adam lamakom* (between ourselves and the Omnipresent) and *ben adam lakhavero* (between ourselves and other people). *Beyn adam lamakom* may require only the minimum structure and restriction in finding one's unique way to fulfill Proverbs 3:6: "In all your ways know Him [God]." However, *beyn adam lakhavero* requires the structure of societies and reverence for other lives. The combination is critical. If we devote ourselves to a superficial view of the realm of *beyn adam lamakom*, our lives become narcissistic and warped. We become alienated from the holiness of all that shares the planet with us. If we focus exclusively on *beyn adam lakhavero*, we let atrophy the deepest dimension of our being. The two realms are interwoven. Given the great value in cultivating both spheres, we can see that both spontaneous and traditional prayer have their place.

All relationships harbor possible problems and potential riches. Whatever issue we address, we need to retain an awareness that we exist on numerous planes simultaneously and that all are vital to what human life entails. If we amputate one sphere of our life, we diminish the majesty of our humanity. This is sometimes done in the name of spirituality, but it tends to merely narrow spirituality rather than enhancing it. Confusion occurs when we apply the thoughts and criteria appropriate to one sphere to another, inappropriate sphere. Recognizing the holiness and Divinity of each sphere and how they coexist and interpenetrate helps to sanctify each sphere and to honor it in a suitable manner.

Language and Silence

Language is essential to who we are as human beings. It is a defining characteristic of human life. Refraining from speech for a period of time can heighten our awareness of both its essential role in our lives and its misuse. Speech is invaluable in communicating emotions, ideas, etc. If someone fasts from speech with the goal of spiritual enhancement they avoid the challenges, potential joys, and even ecstasy that verbal communication can offer. They also deprive others of the gifts they could provide verbally, as well as the peaks to which they could elevate others with their words. On the other hand, fasts of silence can unquestionably contribute to a person's sensitivity to speech. There's a *minhag* (custom) in certain circles of undertaking a fast of silence during the Hebrew month of *Elul* in preparation for the Days of Awe (that is, from Rosh Hashanah through Yom Kippur), which immediately follow *Elul*.

We use language to communicate and connect on many planes of existence. It is probably the dominant tool in the realm of *beyn adam lakhavero*, but it obviously also plays the central role in prayer where it functions primarily *beyn adam lamakom*. Prayer is a complex and subtle endeavor. It would be foolish to be prescriptive about it. Rather, it is important to recognize the usefulness of many forms of prayer, each theoretically appropriate to different understandings and visions of God or particular aspects of connecting to the Eternal One. My concern here is primarily meditative, that is, to look at the sort of prayer that attempts to take us to a state of being with the Divine, sensitizing us to the Divine Presence.

Every language has its own music that is related to, but not limited to, the meanings of the words. The music of language also exists independently of all specific meaning. Some people who might lack enough fluency with a language to be able to enter the words by way of their meaning may still enter them by way of the music of the language itself. This may be a more limited vehicle for our words and prayers, but it remains a vehicle nonetheless. It may connect a person to the musical reverberations of our ancestors, while allowing for our own private intentions to be carried by the music. This was my own experience when I was much younger and my understanding of Hebrew was extremely limited, but my fervor was great. Once I began to learn the language much better, I found that many of the words I had previously read with fervor, but without comprehension, I could no longer use because they did not express my experience of the world and God. On the other hand, however, the words that were consistent with how I experienced things I could now use with much greater *kavana*. There was a trade-off in which I could now enter much more deeply into the words that suddenly stepped forward as far more meaningful, while I had to abandon the words that once served as "training wheels" in my journey towards God.

The meaning and impact of words change over the course of their existence, as does our understanding of the cosmos and our place in it. Since most prayer utilizes language, this obviously affects it. Even the music of words is modified by the "background music" that comes to accompany it, while the background music is modified through the ways that societies evolve. Whatever we do, see, hear, etc. is done, seen, heard, etc. in a particular context. That context affects our perceptions. If we listen to a song that is hundreds of years old, we can't hear it the same way people heard it hundreds of years ago because the context (what I'm calling the "background music") has changed too much. The connotations and associations must change of necessity because the context in which we encounter the music is significantly different. This is certainly equally true of language. At times, for example, we'll find Rashi, the great medieval biblical and Talmudic commentator

(1040–1105), explaining the meaning of a biblical word not only because it may be obscure, but also because its meaning in medieval times may have evolved since its biblical usage. When words no longer sing with the resonance they once possessed because their meanings and connotations have modified, when the background music of societies has changed, and when our understanding of the cosmos and God has evolved, we are confronted with the option of rewriting the prayers to fit our current sensibilities, retaining the original texts untampered with, though less fully embraceable, and/or attempting to discover, inject, or invent new meanings for the original versions.

The tradition has mostly treated inherited texts of prayers as too sacred to modify. There are a number of obvious exceptions, such as the wording of Isaiah 45:7, "*yotzer or u'voray khoshekh, oseh shalom u'voray ra*," exchanging its last two words for "*u'voray et hakol*" in the morning service ("Who forms light and creates darkness, makes peace and creates evil" becoming "and creates everything"). Prayer books from liberal Jewish denominations have taken the liberty to modify a few words here and there from the traditional prayer book. As I said earlier, there is a power implicit in retaining the actual words our ancestors used, which transcends simply preserving the common pursuit of a life engaged with the Divine. However, if those ancient phrases can no longer convey our sensibilities, they may become shells of themselves, museum artifacts we visit regularly, rather than living forces.

The *siddur*, the prayer book, evolved over time, but addition rather than substitution tended to be the rule. Simply being able to formulate "ideologically acceptable" prayers does not retain the poetic and musical component so vital to its effectiveness. We can engage Torah and struggle with it, but the *siddur*, when being used and not studied as text, was not meant to be struggled with in this manner. We thrive from connection to the depth of the past, but we also require resonance with our contemporary sensibilities. If we want to deeply enter the words we pray, we need to truly believe in them. If we don't understand what they mean then the words will be limited in terms of how effective a vehicle they can be. Consistency also facilitates usefulness as a vehicle. Encountering the same words regularly, if they have the breadth, depth, and resilience to support it, enables us to grow by way of them. Each *"kadosh"* ("holy") in Isaiah's formulation *("Kadosh, kadosh kadosh"*; Isaiah 6:3) is asking us to enter it more deeply. When we repeat "YHVH *hu haElohim*" (YHVH is God) seven times at the end of Yom Kippur, we invoke a crescendo of *kavana*, building through each repetition to explode into the final ecstatic blowing of the *shofar*. Canonized words afford us that possibility, if they sustain their meaningfulness and integrity through the evolution of our sensibilities.

Humans are truly *"m'daber"* ("speakers"—the term Maimonides used to categorize humans in explaining the four types of physical existence in the world). Our choice of words influences and affects our *kavana*. Words are tools—in many ways our most powerful ones. Every tool has the ability to be used for construction or destruction, for unifying or dividing. But words can only take us so far—to the point beyond which only silence is sufficiently articulate. And silence, that crucial part of *adam* that is *dom*, is the realm of meditation.

Private and Public Prayer

Private and public prayer provide overlapping yet distinct functions. A state of *devekut* may be more attainable in solitary prayer, but prayer is often a public function in which each voice can potentially raise the communal consciousness and inspire others. Our commitment to community makes public prayer valuable. Traditional prayers connect us to communities outside our immediate circles and beyond our moment in history. Though that may not be a presence that is tangible to us, it can still be a weighty one, even if only psychologically. Everything affects us, whether we are conscious of it or not. The tone of voice of our neighbor in prayer, the specific words, their rhythm, the energy propelling the words, the torrent or pensiveness of each syllable—it all matters.

Private prayer can include, even exclusively, the use of the traditional prayer book, which contains a spectrum of approaches to God—some petitionary, others embodying an intense awareness of the All-Pervasive, All-Embracing One. The *Sh'ma*, in particular, strives for the experience of Oneness. The *V'ahavta* (the first paragraph of the *Sh'ma*) "*mitzvahs*" us to love the Eternal One "with all your heart, with all your soul, and with everything you are." It is written in the perennial present: "I give you this *mitzvah* today," that is, every day.

The *siddur* is filled with juxtapositions of sublime moments framed by moments filled with paternal and monarchical imagery, and rewards and punishments where the All-Embracing, All-Pervasive One is well hidden. Those who find this meaningful—and they are clearly many—are obviously free to engage in this kind of prayer, but those who seek the Immanent and Transcendent One will find a path to the One only in certain selections of the *siddur*.

Participating in a congregation does not necessitate exclusively praying with the same words at the same time as the majority of the congregation. You can enter a realm of private prayer at any moment and return to the group prayer when ready. Each individual's presence matters and each person's devotion affects the atmosphere in the room. It may require extra focus to be able to *daven* at one's own pace in a congregational setting, but if that's what a person needs to do, they should. They are still participating in the community.

A community doesn't require conformity; it requires cooperation and a degree of consensus. Not everyone has to share the same relationship to prayer or have the identical intention and understanding of specific prayers. That would be totally unrealistic. In each individual's evolution, understanding and *kavana* evolve and may change from instance to instance. A community contains a loose consensus of orientation and values; beyond that, its character is formed by the mixture of sensibilities among its members.

One crucial perspective vis-à-vis the traditional prayers, and prayer in general, revolves around the understanding of prayer's function. One pole on the continuum of perspectives is that prayer is a vehicle functioning to facilitate our connection with God. The other pole is that we are there to "serve prayer" in a sense or, more accurately, to conform ourselves to the beliefs and orientations explicit and implicit in the prayers. We have to fulfill the obligation to pray. This latter attitude is consistent with a patriarchal image of God, the anthropomorphic deity who expects obedience from "his" human "creation." This view is inconsistent with the sense of God as *m'malei kol almin* (filling all universes), *sovev kol almin* (encompassing all universes). A deity that demands, tends to demand obedience and requires being "prayed to." In contrast, in meditative prayer we are simply praying, being buoyed, sensitized, and enlivened by the sublime words. But not all prayer must be meditative, even as it is focused on a non-anthropomorphic deity.

Each level of a person has prayer appropriate to it. We may want to articulate our own needs and ideals in prayer—not with the fantasy of an attentive heavenly parent fulfilling them, but, for example, to strengthen our own and our community's commitment to *tikkun olam*, to repairing the world. We may need to articulate our vision and concepts of God (and God in our lives) to help focus and encourage ourselves and others to live consistently with these concepts. Though these methods of prayer may be conducive to a less unitive relationship with God, they can also be in harmony with, and complementary to, prayer that does ultimately seek such union. The concept of meditative prayer is not meant to provide a yardstick against which to critique our own or other people's prayer lives. Rather, it is meant to elucidate prayer as one more very potent tool towards sensitizing us to the Divine that is omnipresent and within which we exist.

The larger our vision of God, the more that God is perceived and experienced as *m'malei kol almin* and *sovev kol almin*, the more prayer enhances our sensitivity to the planet and all that exists here and the more *beyn adam lamakom* (between ourselves and the Omnipresent) translates into *beyn adam lakhavero* (between ourselves and other people). We each filter our culture's language, but through that personal tool we can in turn articulate and promote the harmony and unity of the planet. We can join our voices to the ancient echoes of our ancestors via the words they bequeathed us. There is a great deal of power in those ancient echoes. They voice a common yearning towards the Divine, even when their vision of the Divine is not entirely congruent with our own. When they can be embraced unreservedly because they *do* articulate our own grasp and striving for harmony with the Divine, their impact is all the more potent. It must be added that the more prayer is engaged in consciously, the more *kavana* invested in it, the greater its impact in our lives. This applies to every type of prayer where the words matter. Repeating words that one cannot believe in or understand may have a psychological and social benefit of satisfying the desire to identify with the community and share in its heritage, but it has little to do with prayer as a means of communing with the Divine.

To reiterate, when praying in community, not all prayer must be geared towards a meditative union with God. In the course of a Shabbat service, for example, you can *daven* on various levels, enhancing your connection to the community and still devoting sections to entering the most resonant words as fully as possible.

Meditative Prayer

Ultimately, each utterance is its own reward. The more we can truly inhabit the words, the greater the *kavana* we attain and, therefore, the greater the reward, because that *is* the reward. The words have served as a bridge or vehicle to a communion with the Divine. But the words have to be broad enough to house an expanded consciousness (*mokhin d'gadlut*). Each word has its own ability to house our consciousness. Words of supplication are very confining. They can be expressed with great sincerity and fervor, but they maintain distance. It is one thing to feel negligible because we have glimpsed the overawing Presence of God; it is another to feel this way because we perceive our parent as all-powerful and ourself, in contrast, as totally dependent. This is disempowering and renders our connection to God as such too, rather than binding us to the Source of All Being.

The "reward" of our prayer is the experience of prayer itself. The quality of our connection with the Divine will depend on a combination of factors. The breadth and depth of the words themselves that constitute our prayers, and their ability to catalyze and support an expanded consciousness, figure in heavily. Our own lifelong inner work readies us for each present moment. Our *kavana*, concentration, and consciousness during prayer all play pivotal roles.

Our choice of words is of paramount importance. If we cannot intend them with conviction, our prayer is stilted from the start. We will never be able to truly enter a word unless it is deeply meaningful to us and we can open ourselves to it unreservedly. In contrast to language that communicates surface details, thoughts, or sensory experience, meditative prayer invites us to "become" the words, to live them, for the moments we engage them. Our consciousness must be immersed in the word so that it fills us and is all we intend or "are" for the moments that we become it. In this way, with care-full usage, prayer becomes a meditative activity.[3]

However, meditative prayer is not solely about words. There is a subtle continuum between the music of silence and the music of language. All sound is framed in silence and all silence is framed in sound. Sounds and their accompanying silences together are the full articulation, even when expressed only in our minds. A *davened* word, if entered fully, is a chariot *(merkavah)* for the spirit the more we meld our consciousness to it. As we grow in our ability to experience *kedushah* (holiness) and "*m'lo khol ha'aretz k'vodo*" (the whole earth filled with God's glory), we increase our capacity for living each ample word of prayer and being transported and transformed by it. Just as Maimonides classified humans as "*m'daber*" (speakers), so it is that the more we are able to be and live our highest words, the more fully we realize our humanness. This is not "*m'daber*," the rote mutterer, but "*m'daber*," the "intender," whose words speak most fully. This is another form of *brit milah*, that is, a covenant of the "word" in addition to the covenant of circumcision.[4] Merely mouthing a word is not synonymous with fully intending it. You can let the words "I love you" pass your lips, but this is a very different experience than being filled with those words.

---

3. When I use the term meditation, I don't mean contemplation, where a distance is still sustained between the contemplator and the contemplated. Meditation, in my usage here, strives to transcend any distance.

4. "*Milah*" means both "circumcision" and "word."

Throughout this book, I'm referring to prayer in Hebrew. Though I believe it possible to create prayer in English with the *kishke*-consciousness of Hebrew liturgy, most translations, however necessary in many contexts, are akin to black-and-white photographs of Kandinsky's early color-lush abstractions. Translations tend to lose the music of the original sounds of the words. Every language has its own inherent music, which contributes to its power and meaning.

It is particularly difficult to transmit the music of Hebrew into a language as distinct from it as English. The structure of Hebrew contains a lot of internal rhyme, which often sounds artificial in English. As in the sympathetic resonance of strings of an instrument, the original Hebrew words of prayers often reverberate with biblical verses or allusions to them, which are lost in translation. In addition, the original Hebrew carries the weight of thousands of years of being the instrument of expressing Jewish experience, which no other language could reproduce.

Meditative prayer is about "being," not "doing." It is not prayer in which we "think" about the content of the prayers, but rather prayer in which our goal is to "be" the content of the prayer. We try to lead our consciousness by means of the words of prayer to live as fully as possible the intention of those prayers. We aim to bridge the perceived distance between ourselves and the Divine. One method of attempting this is to hold each word in our consciousness until we become so absorbed that we no longer are aware of the intentional part of the act. We only become aware of it again upon emerging from it.

Just as we exist on various planes simultaneously—for example, as an integral part of the One and as a separate individual living on the emotional, intellectual, spiritual, and physical planes simultaneously—so in each of these dimensions various levels coexist. Our most mature and realized aspect cohabits in each plane with other levels along the continuum to our least realized self. We don't exist in a state of stasis, but in various states of flux. We need to nurture all aspects of ourselves to foster their balance and growth. We want to cultivate the most realized part of each plane, developing our most emotionally mature self and not succumbing to those aspects on the other end of the continuum. We need to keep our prayers sensitive to, and in harmony with, our spiritual, emotional, and intellectual selves. Prayer that infantilizes us rather than fostering our emotional maturity may inhibit the flourishing of our overall humanity and distort our spiritual self because we, as humans, will be out of balance. The same is true of our intellectual selves. If we utilize prayers that lag well behind our intellectual development, we're fostering disharmony between various aspects of ourselves. Our spirituality will be "asymmetrical," as it were, and its growth curtailed.

Hopefully we are always striving to grow, not only to change. Change is inevitable. The world changes and our bodies age. If we maintain a keenness of mind, perception, and spirit, we will evolve spiritually in response to each of life's stages. We don't want to ignore or thwart our emotional health by vilifying ego, but rather we want to grow emotionally by cultivating a mature ego that knows itself as a separate self and can live in harmony with our transcendent self, which knows itself as part of the Infinite One. Returning to the analogy of the whole body with its individual components, we don't want to cut off circulation to any part of the body, but rather we want to keep it all in optimal health.

We also need to recognize that prayer does not have to be, as it were, a one-note melody. Ideally, various types of prayer will appeal to various planes of a person, one complementing the other. Not everyone need do all, or any, of these types of prayer, even if they crave a spiritual lifestyle. Our concern here is the soul of each person and the spiritual health of the community. Where there is coercion, there is a spiritual atmosphere tainted by the myopic view of a mob or of low-consciousness leaders. Truly engaged prayer is a sublime song. We must remain cognizant of the needs of the community and not be exclusively focused on *beyn adam lamakom* (between ourselves and the Omnipresent).

Ultimately *beyn adam lamakom* must include *beyn adam lakhavero* (between ourselves and other people). If our connection to the Divine has not sensitized us to the rest of creation, then our experience of God needs to grow. If we are not sensitized to the rest of creation, then we are not yet experiencing Isaiah's words regarding the Eternal One: "*m'lo khol ha'aretz k'vodo*" (the whole earth is full of God's Glory); rather, we are making an idol (and often an ideology) of our own need for transcendence.

This need for transcendence, like everything else, requires balance. Is balance necessary within each individual or is it primarily necessary in the community as a whole, in which case we would have a "division of labor"? For example, some people who are primarily geared towards the "mechanical" tasks of the physical plane would be balanced on a societal level by those geared towards the less physical plane. No one can force another to sensitize themselves to their emotions, to sharpen their intellect, or to nourish their souls, but it is to each person's benefit that the possibility is there—not through coercion, but by having the safety and sympathetic encouragement that enables it. This also benefits society as a whole.

There is a perpetual tension between balancing the private cultivation of the soul and the public consciousness, between the democratic sensibility to honor the individual and the need to seek the maximum public good. This tension exists on the macrocosmic and microcosmic levels in the apparent dichotomy of the realms of *beyn adam lamakom* and *beyn adam lakhavero*. If an individual has a consciousness of the Divine that finds parts of the traditional *siddur* (prayer book) too limiting spiritually, that need not prevent that individual's participation in the larger community. Rather, this person can either seek out a similarly sensitized alternative community or try to expose and compassionately encourage receptivity to this kind of consciousness in the existing community.

Is a life geared towards cultivating the spiritual always destined to remain a minority pursuit? Is it a messianic pipe dream to imagine the contrary? Perhaps, but like all messianic pipe dreams, it inspires us and encourages us along the path. If your intense prayer experience in the congregation can affect, even minimally, the experience of another and nudge open a door to another level of prayer for that person, you have done something significant both *beyn adam lakhavero* and *beyn adam lamakom.*

Chapter 5

Jewish Meditation

WE CAN'T EXIST IN this world without "doing," but we also can have moments of "being" in which we experience the world in a less distracted, diffused way. This applies to both the "physical" and the "spiritual" universe. Optimally, meditation is an attempt to "be" in as pure a manner as possible and to connect with the Presence that fills the universe. "Doing" and "being" are part of every moment of our lives. So much of our lives can be caught up in "doing" that we lose connection with the "being" component and become detached or oblivious to it. The challenge is how to stay connected to "being" as much as possible despite the difficulty. What techniques or practices facilitate that connection and help us maintain it throughout our days and our lives?

Meditation is a method and practice of engaging the mind to attain a state of awareness and being that bypasses the rational mind's limitations and strives for realms of experience and existence that are *l'malah mekol sekhel (Avodat HaKodesh* 8c by Meir Ibn Gabbai), that is, beyond all rational thought. Through various techniques, meditation can be used to deepen the silence, sensitizing the meditator to the *"kol d'mamah dakah,"* "the subtle sound of silence" (1 Kings 19:12). It is not a process of contemplation because thought and rational inquiry are not involved. Rather, it employs techniques to still the mind and stop its racing from thought to thought or image to image. The technique is described

THE SACRED NOW

in the early mystical text *Sefer Yetzirah* (chapter 1, Mishnah 8): "Restrain your mouth from speaking and your heart [mind] from cogitating, and if your heart [mind] races, return to the Place [to the Omnipresent]. Therefore it is said [Ezekiel 1:14] 'the *khayot* run and return.'" This phrase about the *"khayot"* ("angelic beings," which can also be read as *"khiyut,"* "life force") became, during the course of centuries, an important quotation concerning mystical experience and various states of consciousness that are attainable, but probably not permanently sustainable.

Meditation, like meditative prayer, is essentially about being, not doing. Doing, to some degree or other, is always an expression of our being, of course. All our activities emanate directly or circuitously from the essence of who we are. The more connected to our essential being we are, the more our doing is in harmony with our being. This harmony or lack thereof will fluctuate both during our routine activities and during meditation. When we are most fully being, on the other hand, there's a union of our consciousness with our essence and, therefore, with all Being. Meditation tries to penetrate the partitions between our consciousness and Consciousness, that is, God.

If the consciousness is there, Being permeates any and all activities. This is what was meant by the term "being *nikhnas*" or "entering" an activity, that is, being utterly present in it, rather than having a division in our consciousness. Being *nikhnas* requires that our being fills our doing. Of course, there are innumerable gradations of this state. Our *kavana*, our ability to direct our minds and modify our consciousness, determines to what degree we can be *nikhnas* in any given circumstance.

Meditation is a means of exercising and strengthening *kavana*. The spiritual "muscles" that enable us to focus and enter something more fully are toned by the process of bringing our consciousness back to the *makom*, the Omnipresent, or to the point of focus. We may focus on a phrase of great import that can sustain a deep entering, or a Hebrew letter such as the *aleph*, which reverberates with profound echoes of the Divine Presence, or the *"shem hameforash"* (literally "the explicit Name"), YHVH, as a focal

96

point. We may use an image such as the *ner tamid*, the "Eternal Lamp," which symbolizes the Eternal One. We may attempt to enter a state of *Ayin* or "No-Thingness" directly with no intermediary steps. Generally the process of "*ratzo vashov*" (Ezekiel 1:14), of the mind running (leaving) and returning to focus, will occur. This process enhances our ability to bring *kavana* to any moment and any activity and, over time, to strengthen the intensity of our *kavana*.

Consciousness is not a rational activity. You can comprehend something by thinking about it, but you become conscious of something by being present to it. The more you focus on being present to someone or something, the more you lose consciousness of yourself. You're not thinking about that someone or something in relation to yourself; you're focusing on that someone (or something) in relation to herself, himself, or itself. You open your physical and non-physical senses to encounter another's being as unreservedly as possible.

Can one prove this point logically? Logic is no more the appropriate measure for the meaningfulness of this category of statement than it is for apprehending the grandeur of a Beethoven symphony, a Jackson Pollock masterpiece, or the majesty of the sky. What makes these entities moving or meaningful is not their functionality, but rather their presence and aesthetic eminence, which cannot be reduced to our senses, though we apprehend them via those senses.

Jewish meditation is an attempt to be as present as possible to the Divine Presence. There is no limit to how present we can be to the Infinite One. We can always cultivate a deeper awareness. We can always be more awake. We can *do* things meditatively by bringing great awareness into any activity, but "pure" meditation is the process of trying to open the channels of consciousness to the Omnipresent.

The use of a phrase as a focus of meditation is akin to meditative prayer, with the distinction that in meditation the phrase is generally repeated over and over. One can have two goals with this process. You could use the phrase to bypass rational thought and open up to Presence by repeating the phrase with no attention to meaning, using it as a decoy for the chattering mind. A deeper part of consciousness can surface once the chattering mind is preoccupied elsewhere. On the other hand, you can take a phrase heavily freighted with meaning and enter that phrase with as much *kavana* and attention as possible, slowing it down so that your consciousness resides in the word. If you continue to hold that word effectively, you may eventually leave it like ballast to dwell in No-Thingness.

The Interplay of Being and Doing, Yesh and Ayin

The state of our being influences everything in our life. When we grasp that our actions are consequences of the state of our being, then the cultivation of our being becomes of paramount importance. Connected with this, however, is the fact that every action likewise affects our state of being. Actions taken without conscious *kavana* affect our state of being also, though we have no control over them. The greater our *kavana*, the more we have an effect on our being.

The cultivation of acts of kindness can help sensitize us to the inherent worth of others. If we believe in the potential of people to improve, then we can strive to cultivate true growth of sensitivity and consciousness. A traditional morning prayer expresses this idea: *"Elohai neshama shenatata be, t'hora he"* (My God, the soul that you have given me is pure). Cultivating a connection to that purity is a potential ramification of meditation. Underlying what I'm saying here is a basic affirmation of the sacredness of daily life and of existence itself, including the most seemingly mundane aspects of life. Consciousness is not a matter of comprehending, but of being cognizant of the presence of something. Sensitizing our spiritual senses to the Presence of the Divine is fundamental to Jewish meditation and, ideally, to most ritual activity.

Ritual activity functions on the emotional, psychological, social, and spiritual levels simultaneously. All levels matter and together provide a balance in a person's life. Each level influences the others, for they interpenetrate and are interdependent.

The realm of *Yesh*, of differentiation and "individuality," is sacred, but that is only part of the larger picture. It is filled and unified by the realm of *Ayin* (No-Thingness). It is obscuring the obvious to deny the existence of the realm of *Yesh*. However, affirming its reality does not mean that our conventional perceptions of it are accurate. Our consciousness affects our perception of the realm of *Yesh*.

Withdrawal from the world is not a superior, "holier" way of being. It is an escape from the great project of living this finite existence with an awareness of the Infinite that suffuses it. It is an escape from the Divinity that fills everything. "Choose life" (Deuteronomy 30:19) is consistent with (though, obviously, not synonymous with) experiencing transcendence simultaneously in the very details of the world of immanence, that is, tasting the eternal in the ephemeral.

Transcendence is not going "beyond" the realm of *Yesh*, but rather going so deeply into the realm of *Yesh* that you both recognize and honor it while also experiencing it as part of the non-dualistic nature of *Ayin*. In other words, transcendence is experiencing the transcendent permeating the realm of *Yesh*, not negating it.

Consciousness of Nothingness

Meditation, no matter how it's understood, is always a tool, but to what end? This question, to a degree, differentiates various orientations toward meditation. Guided visualizations, contemplation, and focused thinking tend to foster separation and, therefore, aren't geared towards a consciousness of *Ayin* (which is a state of non-duality). Of course, there are forms of meditation that don't fit into the above categories and still don't veer towards *Ayin* because that is not the spiritual worldview of the practitioners. Nevertheless, they may accidentally emerge into a state of *Ayin* like a traveler deviating from, or lacking, an itinerary may emerge upon totally unexpected wonders.

The inner compass of guided visualizations, contemplation, etc. is different from that of meditation that seeks to transcend all distance between *Yesh* and *Ayin*. Guided visualization has much more in common with meditative prayer than with *Ayin*-oriented meditation. The words reach their meditative peak upon our entering, lingering with, and dwelling in them, the ultimate summit being approachable with the explicit Divine Name, YHVH. The meditative moment is when we enter the word and ultimately transcend it. The word is a springboard towards what it "represents." *Ayin* is the ultimate source of the Divine Name (and of everything else too, of course).

If *Ayin* is the ultimate source of everything, then shouldn't everything and anything be an equally potent focal point for meditation? In one sense the answer is "yes," because the Divine is *m'malei kol almin*, filling all universes. In another sense, however, the Divine Name, unencumbered by pronunciation and attempting the seemingly paradoxical goal of referring to the interpenetrating of the Transcendent God and the Immanent God, is the most explicit sign and symbol and, therefore, potential bridge to *Ayin* that we have in the universe of *Yesh*.

When the "explicit" Divine Name *(shem hameforash)* is the focus of meditation, this implies that the Name itself becomes the springboard for approaching *Ayin*. If we "contemplate" the Name, we maintain our separateness through contemplating an "other." The Name itself begins as an "other," as long as we maintain that distance of using it to address an "other." However, when we use the name as an entity that we become absorbed by through opening our consciousness to it, rather than by thinking about it or contemplating it, it becomes a gateway to *Ayin*-consciousness. It is the "word" most pregnant with significance while still functioning in the realm of *Yesh*. It is the most powerful expression of the apparent paradox of *Ayin* infusing the realm of *Yesh*, that is, of No-Thingness penetrating and vivifying all of Some-Thingness. Therefore, when the *shem hameforash* (YHVH) is the sole focus of consciousness and we are able to be so absorbed by it as to lose all sense of "who" is being lost, the Name becomes a conduit for consciousness of *Ayin*.

The unutterability of the *shem hameforash*, the Explicit Name (of God), is the bridge between humans as "*m'daber*" (speaker) and humans as inhabitants of the dominion of "*dom*," silence. It is also the bridge between the transcendent and immanent "faces" of God. We have a word, a name, comprised of letters and yet it cannot be given voice. Every attempt to utter it would be to diminish it. Those who struggle to surmise the original pronunciation of the Name very much miss this point.

Consciousness of *Ayin* compels without "commanding." "Commanding" comes from a "voice" from the realm of *Yesh*, the voice of an external judging authority. The consciousness of *Ayin*, which is an experience *beyn adam lamakom* (between humans and the Omnipresent), compels a reverence for the realm of *beyn adam lakhavero* (between humans).

When one has a sense of *Ayin*, it is experienced as an encounter with the Infinite—there is no differentiation or boundary. Boundaries imply finiteness as well as differentiation, whereas a sense of no boundaries, no limits, no object or subject beginning and ending, carries an air of the Infinite. When the tradition forbids the making of an image or the uttering of the explicit Name, it's creating an atmosphere and culture conducive to *Ayin* consciousness. When we engage in meditation that seeks to experience *Ayin*, it requires a lack of any image, word, or symbol, or, in turn, a word, image, or symbol that serves as a gateway by essentially focusing the consciousness and subsequently falling away.

All imagery is from the realm of *Yesh*, of *olam haperud*, the universe of (apparent) differentiation and, therefore, of separation. Even if we recognize *Ayin* in *Yesh*, it is idolatrous to treat any aspect of the realm of *Yesh* as the focus of our devotion. We seek union and communion with the One, the All-Encompassing, All-Pervasive One. Even worshiping one of the Divine Emanations, that is, one of the *Sephirot*, is considered idolatry in the eyes of the tradition.

Ayin doesn't negate the realm of *Yesh* but, rather, illuminates what unifies, underlies, and fills it. It highlights the eternal in the ephemeral. It is the equivalent of shifting focus from the microscopic to the macrocosmic, or discovering the inner world of the body that literally vivifies it but is not apparent when looking at the surface of the skin. It is the invisible sun illuminating a breathtaking moon. It is like the gravitational pull of love that sets so much else in motion.

The False Dichotomy of Secular and Spiritual

Conventionally, the realm of *Yesh* finds its clearest embodiment in physical and secular existence. However, when "secular" activities are characterized as the antithesis of spiritual pursuits, a false dichotomy is fostered in people's minds. This contributes to the evisceration of the spiritual core of our daily activities and renders them more prone to being perceived on a primarily material level, making them ever more susceptible to commercial exploitation and superficiality. This also artificially empowers a small class of "religious" professionals and institutions by fostering an aura of "spiritual" superiority among the clergy while offering up to the "priests" of commercialism the majority of society for material exploitation.

Power in human society is thus divided up between a commercial province and an ecclesiastical sphere of influence, both of which are hierarchically structured. Our bodies and our souls are conveniently divorced from each other, one to be preyed upon by (or subject to) the religious ruling elite and the other by the business elite. The hierarchical structure of "religious" institutionalism is supported by the spiritual evisceration of secular life, which again makes people more vulnerable to commercialism. All of this has little to do with God, but everything to do with the allocation of, and struggle for, power, control, and influence in society. The monarchical, hierarchical paradigms for sacred metaphors reinforce these attitudes and structures.

Religious "authorities" and beliefs that negate the holiness of daily secular life consolidate and exacerbate the divisions to which modern society is subject. We are left with the common dichotomy in which an embrace of modernity and secular society is generally accompanied by a diminished pursuit of the spiritual, and traditional religious attitudes seem increasingly irrelevant to modern life (even though fundamentalist practitioners exploit some of the technological advances of modernity) and tend to attract socially and intellectually conservative people.

A radical democracy of the spirit affirms the sacredness of daily life and the infusion of secular activity with a palpable Divinity, given the requisite consciousness. This doesn't mean that any and all secular activity is sacred, but that secular life, lived in a conscious manner, is inherently no less sacred than any other activity.

Balancing Yesh and Ayin

When I was about seventeen years old I was very attracted to Chabad and spent a lot of time with Lubavitchers. I remember hearing a story about the *Alter Rebbe* (Shneur Zalman, the founder of Chabad) in which his Hasidim are waiting for him to begin Kol Nidre and he's nowhere to be found. Later they learn that he had gone to take care of a poor widow who was in need of wood and food to feed her five children, and that took priority.

Ideally we need to balance a quest for *Ayin* with a healthy dose of commitment to the realm of *Yesh*. Rather than occupying ourselves exclusively with pursuing the transcendent, we generally need to be well grounded in our very concrete physical needs. Otherwise, how can we be compassionate listeners and fully engaged companions? There would be an implicit arrogance in listening from one's perch on some "transcendent" plane. One of the great strengths of the classic Hasidic Rebbes was their apparent intimacy with the worlds of both *Ayin* and *Yesh*, by way of which they guided and cared for their Hasidim. They could love their followers as real flesh-and-blood people, not distantly or abstractly. People deserve to be truly recognized as equals. If, additionally, one can perceive the Divine in others, how much the better! It is an easy formula to spout, but how hard to achieve!

If we are capable to any degree of perceiving the eternal in the ephemeral, then being truly open to another person means also being present to the eternal in them, not merely listening deeply to the realm of *Yesh* that they embody. Both deserve to be engaged meaningfully, which requires not confusing them by relating to one realm with the sensibilities appropriate to the other. If we try to be fully present to another, it is necessary to minimize the degree to which our own selves distract us and shade our perceptions of the other. There's an element of "*bittul*" (self-nullification) that occurs when we are totally open to another, when we are present to them as entirely as possible. In addition to those elements that they consciously intend to convey, we may perceive and be present to elements they are not aware of communicating.

On the purely *Yesh* level, there are various components of listening. For example, we listen to the literal meanings of the words another expresses, but we also need to listen to the "music" of the words that contextualize and modify them. There is a visual component of listening that requires attentiveness to facial and physical gestures accompanying the music and lyrics, as it were, of another's speech. There is an analogous kind of listening in the realm of *Ayin*. Meditation is an exercise in listening or trying to tune into the realm of *Ayin*, which is only feasible during silent meditation. Everything in the universe of *Yesh* is also part of the unity of *Ayin*, so everything is both part of the wholeness, the oneness, the non-dual nature of *Ayin*, while simultaneously a unique manifestation or expression of *Ayin* in the realm of *Yesh*. From the perspective of the uniqueness of each individual, there is a piece of the One of which only she, he, or it is privileged to partake. To thoroughly experience both one's uniqueness as an individual and one's transcendent nature is to realize one's full being, which is the spiritual analog of "maturity" on the psychological, emotional, and intellectual planes. This is more of a process than a destination. This evolving state develops at disparate rates in the various aspects of different individuals.

A key characteristic marking "maturity" is a finely tuned inner compass, as opposed to an external "voice" directing a person. One's moral maturity is one's inner grasp of good. One's intellectual maturity is one's ability to think, learn, and discern. There is an analogous spiritual maturity that meditation can help cultivate by refining one's inner senses.

Practicing Meditation

In this inspirited physical universe, everything is in flux and motion. The mind is rarely static and operates on various levels simultaneously. As with prayer, meditation takes numerous forms and techniques and is not limited to one purpose. Just as the mind operates on various levels simultaneously, we *live* simultaneously on various levels. Ideally these levels are in harmony with one another, though sometimes they are very dissonant. One level or realm will affect all others. The nature, quality, and depth of our spiritual life, for example, will influence the way we experience the realms of the senses.

The difference between hearing certain sounds as noise and as music is analogous. We might hear the sounds of nature or machines as song, or we might not. No sound is free from the social and cultural associations that affect the nuances of our hearing. Nor can we isolate any act or state of being completely from the numerous associations accompanying it. Every act, every state of being, and every word we utter or think has innumerable layers in which we can inhabit or experience it. Every act has the potential to deepen our state of consciousness. The deeper the state of consciousness, in turn, the more sensitized we are to the greater depths of the acts and words themselves. Meditation is a formidable path for living on, and being sensitized to, those deeper layers of everything we say or do, but nothing guarantees this immediate outcome. Rather, it requires a lifelong cultivation for which meditation can be an invaluable tool. But meditation is not the only tool, and perhaps it will always remain a minority pursuit.

It would be presumptuous to assume that what is most meaningful to some people should be most meaningful to all others as well. When I was very young I felt very messianic about "mysticism." I believed that anyone exposed to meditation and mysticism would find their life completely changed. Over the more than forty years that I have tried to teach it in one form or another, it's become more than obvious that it truly isn't for everyone. There are many people for whom it does not resonate at all. We shouldn't confuse *a* path with *the* path. In the same way, we shouldn't blur the distinctions between description and prescription. There are many different forms of meditation and ultimately they probably function best and are most suitable to different personality types. As one becomes more conversant and better oriented in the terrain, he/she must ascertain what works best for him/her.

One of the challenges of a democratic spiritual sensibility is to maintain the balance between recognizing the validity of various paths and living with the necessary disciplined commitment to one's own values and vision. There is something comforting and facile in having an external authoritative voice determining one's choices and asserting infallibility in those decisions, even when they are very demanding. Recognizing the viability of different paths includes acknowledging that regardless of how valuable meditation might be, and how "ultimate" an experience union with the Divine is, not everyone need pursue it. And though there are multiple goals people seek via meditation, my own orientation of seeking a state of *devekut*, or union, with the Divine likely biases my perception of other orientations. It's a truism to me that the All-Encompassing, All-Pervasive One is perennially perceptible, but in order to attain that experience we must attune our spiritual faculties to it. Meditation is one of our most powerful tools towards that end.

The orientation and "belief system" held by a person generally influence the outcome of their spiritual pursuits (though there are exceptions, for example, where someone's sudden and unexpected vision and experience overturn those very beliefs). If someone holds an anthropomorphic idea of God, for example, their prayer and meditation life will reflect that and be severely limited by it. It is comparable to one's seeking the solace of parental protection and security and thereby stunting one's emotional and psychological growth. Of course, during the childhood and adolescent stages of a person's development, parental protection is appropriate, but hopefully at a certain point the inner resources for independence are at least latent and, consequently, realizable. If ignored, the habits of dependence become more formidable and harder to outgrow. This is true vis-à-vis independence in one's intellectual life, emotional independence in one's psychological growth, and in one's spiritual development as well. A religion that stigmatizes those who deviate from a narrow arena of "approved" beliefs stunts spirituality and promotes an implicit lack of confidence in the inner resources of its adherents.

Reading Our Texts

Nevertheless, a religion may be founded upon sacred writings that contain (in part) the inspired words of those who have traversed the path in the past and expressed it through the inevitable filters of language and the generally prevailing *Weltanschauung* of their era, even if they transcended it to some degree. This does not mean that seeking spiritual inspiration is the only valid way of reading of Scripture. The Bible is such a vast body of "literature" and insight that it lends itself to various fruitful readings and orientations. Each of those readings has its valid sphere. Confusion occurs when applying the standards and lens of one realm of reading on those of another realm of reading.

When we confuse the "*sod*" (mystical/esoteric) reading of the Torah with the more obvious "*pshat*" (literal, plain) reading of it, we constrict a valid reading of the text. Possibly in the past people superimposed one realm of reading on another "in good faith," but it's no longer possible to do so and maintain intellectual integrity regarding the *pshat*. This doesn't mean, however, that a mystically inspired reading has no validity. If it's undertaken in full acknowledgment that it doesn't supersede other levels of reading the text, but rather coinhabits the universe of the text, it can both inspire and be undertaken "in good faith." Analogously, what a painter puts into a canvas doesn't restrict the inspiration that viewers may draw from it. When we see the grain of the canvas embedded in the paint and value its presence in the work, this doesn't negate the more obvious pictorial qualities that the painting surface depicts. When one sees the power of the ocean underlying the immediate phenomenon of a wave absorbed into the shore, one doesn't contradict the other. When we hear the drama of the human condition in the simple sounds of an infant wanting food, affection, or attention, we perceive a great reality that's not explicit in the literal expressions, but nevertheless is palpable in them.

In the same way that every "creator" generally expresses her or his vision through the filters of language and prevailing *Weltanschauung*, every reader or spectator likewise perceives the expression through their own filters (of course "language" can also take visual, musical, or other forms). Only in the realm of No-Thingness, of *Ayin*, where we enter a sphere of no language or image such as that which we seek in certain meditative states, may we transcend this. However, once we attempt to articulate this experience in any manner, we immediately reenter the domain of the strictures of our age. These strictures may be somewhat flexible, but they're primarily fixed. Of course, existing within the confines of our times, we inevitably have a limited perspective through which to critique our own skewed perceptions. The elasticity of our strictures can afford us a glimpse at our limitations, but every glimpse, every insight, and every attempt at expression is rooted in the intellectual and spiritual technologies, ideologies, and psychologies of the times. Even the experience of *Ayin*, of No-Thingness, is constrained by the same constellation of forces always in operation in all human communication once we seek to articulate the experience. Yet *Ayin* remains in the marrow of all *Yesh*, accessible through meditation, meditative consciousness, and the grace of unexpected insight.

Ayin remains accessible, but once we reenter the realm of differentiation, our vision of our own experience becomes filtered.

Just as a state of *devekut* vanishes once one has the distance to recognize it, so our comprehension of the experience is inevitably compromised by the limitations of personality. "Comprehension" is a product of distance, whereas "consciousness" is a product of being present. One can never truly "comprehend" *Ayin*, but one can attain a consciousness of it. Meditation is a tool for this.

Cultivating Our Inner Compass

Cultivating our inner compass doesn't necessitate going far from where others have pointed, but deciding in advance where it is free to go is very restricting. We have the ability to undergo spiritual experiences and, subsequently, to critique those experiences, trying to determine how, and if, they can be incorporated into our lives. Meditation can sensitize us to the elements of the tradition that promote social cohesion at the expense of inner growth, but it can also enhance Jewish practices by enabling us to view them, and live them, both with increased sensitivity to the Divine Presence and intensified *kavana*. It can render inadequate the "conventional" synagogue practices that thwart *kavana* by seeking conformity and comfortable common denominators; it can sharpen our spiritual "tools" for infusing our ritual life and synagogue participation with greater *kavana*, yet bring into relief many rote aspects that retard inner growth.

Aesthetic sensibilities have much in common with spiritual sensibilities, deepening one's inner life and sensitivity to the nonmaterial dimensions of existence. In cultivating our aesthetic sensibilities we may try to expose ourselves to the worlds' great aesthetic achievements, hoping to learn how to perceive with increased insight and sharpness. There is a parallel experience in the spiritual realm. Meditation, for instance, is a kind of "looking" and "seeing" with one's inner eye.

A major part of learning to "look" is to give ourselves the luxury of doing so. Allowing ourselves regular periods of meditation, learning various methods of practice, and not pressuring ourselves to come up with "results" are all important. Part of "seeing," externally and internally, is a matter of strengthening our focus. In physical activity, greater tone and flexibility allow for increased endurance and greater focus. So too with meditation: learning to bring one's mind back to the letters of the Divine Name, for example, can enable one to strengthen one's focus. We cannot force the experience; we can merely cultivate it by exercising it and putting our inner eye into a position in which it is present to inner dimensions. Just as with "external" physical seeing, we may continue to look at something and suddenly discover ourselves seeing it in a wholly different way. None of our senses, of course, are exclusively "external"—every perception is processed through our "inner" senses. The three-dimensional world can acquire additional, less tangible but still palpable dimensions beyond the strictly sensual.

All our senses register the concretely sensory components of our experiences, but each experience registers also in the complex inner world of intellect, emotion, and spirit, all of which trespass onto each other's domains. We can only define them in broad strokes because they're not quantifiable, but we can cultivate them through our inner work.

Each act of consciousness and *kavana* influences all subsequent acts. Just as a well-toned body generally finds it easier to engage in physical activity and a well-trained eye more readily sees what is not as apparent to a less-trained eye, so a "well-toned" consciousness more easily enters states of *kavana* and deeper realms of awareness. Each act and state of consciousness affects subsequent ones, and the more we live with *kavana*, rather than unconsciously, the more we cultivate our "being."

There is no possibility of separating our "doing" from our "being." If we act unconsciously, we dull our being. If we act with *kavana* and attempt to refine our moral and spiritual sensibilities, it is always possible to grow into greater depth. Meditation "exercises" a crucial part of our being, but so do moral acts and acts of love, compassion, and kindness. They all complement one other.

Living with commitment but without absolute and rigid answers is challenging. We live in a time of human evolution filled with changes that are more than merely technological. These changes provide new perspectives into what it means to be human, as does the existence of heterogeneous cultures. Fundamentalism militates towards homogeneity and narrows our insights, banishing subtlety and nuance with the false security of pat answers. But for the sake of our individual and collective growth we need the very opposite. It is in the *insecurity* of acknowledging the inevitability of change, and consequent adjustment in direction, that we can grow spiritually. The eternal and immutable *Ayin* constantly interrelates with and penetrates the ever-evolving *Yesh*. One without the other impoverishes our existence.

Jewish meditation, like the mystical tradition from which it emanates, embodies a powerful, and possibly volatile, tool in the quest to live with a higher consciousness. Because it is a potential means of attaining immediate experience of God, rather than a "belief" in God, it can supply experiences that challenge and draw into question our inherited beliefs. It simultaneously hearkens back to the truly fundamental aspect of any religion—the encounter with the Divine—while potentially challenging all organized hierarchical religions by implicitly claiming that anyone can feasibly know God without the mediation of sanctioned representatives of tradition. Jewish meditation, both because it stands outside the highly ritualized structure of the tradition and because it is an intensely private endeavor, is usually perceived as far from the "normative" tradition. This may make it appear threatening to those who see themselves as "guardians" of the tradition, yet it affords great opportunities for reinvigorating Judaism in both traditional and non-traditional ways. It can literally revitalize the tradition by making God a living Presence rather than an exhausted concept. The challenge then becomes: how do we incorporate that experience and/or its residue into our daily and community lives? To this task, Judaism, of whatever stripe, must prove itself equal, or else risk losing some of its most spiritually oriented adherents.

Transcendent Consciousness and Sense of Self

Being fully human requires living consciously on many planes—physical, emotional, psychological, intellectual, and spiritual. Rather than negate each other, these planes interpenetrate one another. The realm of *Yesh*, of individuation, is not illusory, but sacred. Simultaneously, it is unified and permeated with the non-duality of *Ayin*. We strive to perceive the *Ayin* in the *Yesh*, the infinite in the finite, the eternal in the ephemeral. All spiritual rituals should optimally be oriented towards cultivating, communicating, and expressing a reverence for the sacredness of life and the spiritual dimensions that infuse all life. Of course this doesn't mean these rituals cannot also operate on other planes of our existence.

Meditation is a powerful tool, but not the only tool, for cultivating such consciousness. Meditation does not replace action in the world; rather it supplements and informs our ways of being and acting. All actions have their components in all of the various human planes. Meditation is an activity that attempts to cultivate pure "being," that is, it is an example of "doing" that veers towards pure "being." Spiritual exercises such as meditation can lend a more focused, intentional consciousness to the whole of our lives, in both the physical and non-physical realms.

Meditation as its Own Reward

Though we may desire to be in a state of union with God via meditation, meditation is its own reward and in no way guarantees any end "results." It may lead to powerful spiritual moments and experiences, but the practice justifies itself. This is analogous to cultivating one's aesthetic sensibilities, which hopefully provide one with the ability to perceive more profoundly with no other end than perceiving more profoundly. This is the difference between seeing meditation and one's spiritual life as a process and imposing a goal-orientation perspective upon it: it is the act of meditation as a consistent component of one's life that is its own goal and reward. Hopefully it will enhance our ability to "be" more deeply, to fathom, and ultimately experience, the Immanent and Transcendent One with greater sensitivity. Working on one's aptitude for "being" more fully is a perpetual process, not an end point.

Seeking "rewards" for our spiritual and/or religious activity is another ramification of the goal orientation fostered by the commercial underpinnings of society and supported by a hierarchical metaphorical religious worldview. When one's labor, the majority of most people's investment of energy, is geared towards producing a product and/or acquiring the means of purchasing other products, one's normal orientation is towards specific end goals. Rewards and punishments of sorts are very concrete and ubiquitous. Activity is far from being its own reward and is almost strictly a means towards a very tangible end. Similarly, when we relate to God as to a celestial parent or monarch, not only does it infantilize us spiritually, but it usually implies God's rewarding and punishing "his" children or subjects, which is the quality of relationships engendered with "authority" figures. When we perceive the Divine as *m'malei kol almin* and *sovev kol almin*, every act that enhances our connection to God is clearly its own reward and every act that distances us is its own punishment.

Conclusion

In *Pirkei Avot* 1:17 it says, "*lo hamidrash ha-ikar, ela hama'aseh*" (It's not the theory, or study, that is the main point, but the practice). Concepts or beliefs don't necessarily transform people's lives. Even sublime experiences or visions that alter our perceptions don't always translate into concrete changes in the way we actually live. However, in addition to altering our perceptions, we can make our lives an altar, a sanctuary.

In the book of Exodus, the construction of the *mishkan*, the Tabernacle, is described with great precision. The root of this word for "tabernacle" shares its root *(shin, kaf, nun)* with the word *Shekhina*, the Divine Presence. The *mishkan* was seen as the nexus of communication and communion with the Divine. If one perceives or believes that we house the Divine within us, shouldn't we similarly treat our own beings, including our bodies, reverently? I don't mean adorning them in order to distract us from the Divine, or worshipping them idolatrously, but treating them with profound respect—nurturing our minds, honoring and refining our emotions, learning to read them and live harmoniously with them, and promoting the health and fitness of our bodies. If we act respectfully towards buildings as houses of worship, we should certainly act respectfully towards the current homes of our very souls!

The manner in which we live can honor or desecrate the Divine. What might it mean in practice to treat one's life as an altar or sanctuary? First, it implies a reverence for life. Think of the meticulous care the Torah demands concerning the rituals and sacrifices brought to the altar and the preparation required. Though much of it appears to be constructed with an eye towards appeasing an often peevish deity, later commentators spoke of the term *korban*, "sacrifice" (which contains the root *kuf, resh, bet*, implying "bringing near"; *l'hakriv*, which is the verb for "to sacrifice," literally means "to bring near"), as having the ultimate intention of drawing one closer to God. Though we may romanticize the inner lives of our biblical ancestors by superimposing upon them a view of God and the cosmos comparable to our own, clearly the realm of the physical was very spiritually charged for them.

Our insights transform our lives when we embody them, for our bodies house memories too. Following Resh Lakish's statement in *Bereshit Rabba* 47:6, in Kabbalistic and Hasidic literature, the *avot*, the "patriarchs," are spoken of as "being" the *merkavah* (the Divine Chariot), as their lives became vehicles for conveying consciousness of the Divine into the world. Though our consciousness transforms all that we say or do, it can become easier to summon if we embed it in our body's memory. Similarly, our consciousness can enhance community when encoded in communal rituals. But it can also be buried or suffocated by rituals if they cease to be understood as serving consciousness.

Ezekiel's Vision

The opening chapter of the book of Ezekiel contains the original vision of the *merkavah*. I'd like to offer a few passages to illustrate how one can read this vision as a depiction of spiritual transformation. The book of Ezekiel (1:1) begins by saying he was in the midst of exile on the river *k'var* when the heavens opened and he saw visions of God. The phrase "heavens opened," in the passive voice, expresses a sense of the gift or grace of the experience. The prophet's name is "*Yekhezkel* son of *Buzi*"—*Yekhezkel* meaning

115

"God will strengthen," and *Buz* meaning "scorn," "shame," or "contempt." What a combination of names! *Yekhezkel* son of *Buzi* evokes transformation in that out of *Buzi* (my scorn or shame) *Yekhezkel* (God's strength) emerged.

In verse four we find the expression, *"ruakh s'arah ba'ah min hatzafon,"* conventionally translated as "a storm wind came from the north." But *"ruakh s'arah"* could also mean a stormy or tumultuous spirit. And where does it come from? *"Tzafon,"* the north. But *"tzafon"* has the same root and spelling as *"tzafun,"* which means "hidden." And where did this vision of the *merkavah* occur? On the river *k'var. K'var* also means "already," implying that this presence was already there, though it was *"tzafun,"* that is, hidden from him. He was in exile by the river *k'var.* The root of *merkavah,* "chariot," is *resh, kaf, bet,* which contains the same root letters in a different order as the name of the river where the tumultuous experience of his visions occurred.

I would like to read this as a kind of spiritual alchemy. The change in the order of the root letters implies transformation, the emergence of the extraordinary out of the ordinary in which it always resides but is not visible until the heavens open, as it were. This spiritual alchemy is poetically captured by the changing order of root letters, implying inner transformation. Other examples are transforming *"nega"* (*nun, gimmel, ayin*; plague, punishment) to *"oneg"* (*ayin, nun, gimmel*; pleasure, delight), *"pesha"* (*peh, shin, ayin*; transgression) to *"shefa"* (*shin, peh, ayin*; abundance, Divine emanation), and *"rah"* (*resh, ayin*; bad, evil) to *"er"* (*ayin, resh*; wakefulness). If you try to expound upon these transformations using linear thinking, they appear preposterous. Grammatically, words with identical root letters in different orders have nothing in common. Symbolically, however, a powerful teaching is evoked. The letters, which are mythically depicted as the building blocks of creation, convey our ability to fundamentally modify our inner natures.

The same essential insight is repeatedly paraphrased. Earlier we saw it phrased in *Pirkei Avot* 6:2 as "every day a *Bat Kol*, a Divine Voice, emanates from *khorev* [that is, Sinai]." In other words, revelation is always potentially present. In the morning prayers it's written, "*atah m'khadesh b'khol yom tamid ma'aseh v'reshit*" (You [God] perpetually renew creation). The extraordinary is hidden in the ordinary. It is a matter of our ability to perceive it. As Isaiah 6:3 put it, "The whole earth is filled with God's *kavod* [Glory]." Or as the "*modim anakhnu lakh*" ("we thank/acknowledge You") section near the end of the *Amidah* prayer phrases it, "For Your miracles that are with us daily." The issue is twofold: how to attain the vision and how to retain the vision.

How does one attain the experience of God's Glory filling everything or of the miraculous being ever present? You cannot force that perception. It seems to occur as depicted in Ezekiel "*nift'khu hashamayim*" (the heavens open); we suddenly experience the Eternal pervading the ephemeral. The "miraculous" here is not a supernatural event, but a perception of the extraordinary in the ordinary, just as the sense of *kedusha* (holiness) implies something set apart—in this case, the perception of the extraordinary in the ordinary transcends the mundane, the pedestrian. We can prepare ourselves for that vision, if it should come, and strive to retain its impact through attempting to sanctify our lives, embody our insights, and seek to maintain *kavana* in our actions and words. We can seek out and/or develop a community of like-minded people and try to always be able to honestly answer the perennial question addressed to *Adam*, to each human being, "*ayeka*?" ("Where are you?"; Genesis 3:9), with "*hineni*" ("Here I am"; Genesis 22:11; 46:2, Exodus 3:4, etc.), remaining as present as possible.

"Avodah B'Gashmiyut"— Embodying Our Spirituality

To be fully present as humans means to cultivate our spirituality in our human bodies with our emotions and intellects, not despite them. "*Kavana*" is being wholly engaged and not dispassionate, in order to encounter the holy. As it says, "*ivdu et YHVH b'simkha*," "Worship God with joy" (Psalm 10:2). Not only is idol worship a perennial danger, but so is *idle* worship. It is too easy for ritual to turn routine, for people to become numbers, for numbers to lose their magic, and for magic to become sleight of hand and not the vision of the extraordinary in the ordinary.

All content requires form and all form requires content. There is no "disembodied" *kavana*. Whatever insights we attain, we may retain them, that is, call them back to consciousness, by anchoring them in our body through conscious activity. The structure of the *mitzvot* is an excellent model for this as long as they remain means and don't degenerate into ends in themselves.

Avodah b'gashmiyut, embodied worship, can help one keep a balanced vision of the simultaneous realities of the One and its numberless components. The *Sh'ma* and its accompanying paragraphs encode the core of this understanding and practice. In the Babylonian Talmud, Tractate *Brakhot* commences with a discussion of the earliest time it is appropriate to recite the morning *Sh'ma*. The rabbis concluded that the first time for the recitation should be when the *p'til t'kheylet*, the blue cord that was on the *tzitzit* (the fringe of the *tallit*, the prayer shawl), could be distinguished in natural light from the more numerous white threads (of the *tzitzit*). The *Sh'ma*, of course, is the central Jewish prayer professing the Oneness of God. In other words, as soon as we can perceive duality, we profess Unity. The Transcendent One is the Immanent One (some Kabbalistic commentators see this depicted in the letters of the Explicit Name, YHVH, itself) and we will strive to stay aware of the Transcendent in the Immanent and the Immanent in the Transcendent.

"*Sh'ma*" not only means "hear," but also "understand," as in the phrase "*na'aseh v'nishma*," "we will do and we will [consequently] understand" (Exodus 24:7). "Understand" here doesn't mean to have a cerebral comprehension of something, but rather to understand experientially, viscerally. When this awareness occurs, we will (naturally) love YHVH with all our heart, with all our soul, and with all that we are. I'd like to read the next verse differently from its conventional translation: "And these words that *Anokhi* gives you as a *mitzvah* today shall be upon your hearts." Earlier we noted that "*Anokhi*," the first word of the Decalogue, implies the most intense Presence of God. This experience of "*Anokhi*" gives the *mitzvah*. In other words, if you experience "*Anokhi*"—that intense, immense Presence—you are swept up in the One and feel compelled to love the Divine, affirm life, and live harmoniously with creation.

The Torah continues saying, "*v'shinantam l'vanekha*," "you shall repeat these words to and for your children" (Deuteronomy 6:7). Engaging in "*shinun*" (the gerund form of *v'shinantam*), oral repetition, which is a reasonable Hebrew equivalent of the Eastern word "mantra," will help you to teach your children. This root was also employed in relation to the Mishnah, the earlier stratum of the Talmud, which was taught through oral repetition. I'd like to read the phrase "*b'shivt'kha b'vetekha*" as a term for meditation, meaning "when you dwell within yourself," as in the expression "*mibayit u'mikhutz*," "within and without" (Genesis 6:14). So "*b'vetekha*" can be read as "within yourself." You shall utter these words of the *Sh'ma*, repeating them over and over when you dwell within yourself, that is, when you meditate. The passage proceeds to speak of more ways of embodying these words that are the basis of the practices of *tefillin* and *mezuzot*.

The third paragraph of the *Sh'ma*, which is comprised of Numbers 5:37–41, speaks about the practice of wearing *tzitzit*, the fringes put on four-cornered garments, which evolved into the custom of the *tallit*, a four-cornered prayer shawl adorned with *tzitzit* on each corner. Of course, the ancients spoke of the four corners of the earth and the four elements, while medieval Kabbalists spoke of the four "worlds" of *Atzilut* (Emanation), *B'riah* (Creation), *Yetzirah* (Formation) and *Asiyah* (Action). The word "*tzitzit*" may come from "*hetzitz*" (to look), as used in the Talmudic story of the four who entered the "*pardes*," the "orchard," that represented mystical experience and knowledge and evoked echoes of the Garden of Eden or Paradise. In medieval times the term "*pardes*" came to represent the four levels of comprehending the Torah—*p'shat* (literal, simple), *remez* (implied, hinted), *drash* (homiletic), and *sod* (esoteric, secret)—and connoted mystical illumination. So the Torah speaks of seeing the *tzitzit* and thus remembering and doing the *mitzvot* in order to "be holy."

All of this brings us back to an earlier discussion of *kedusha*, holiness, as consciousness of the extraordinary in the ordinary. This quality of awareness is the "Divine Voice that emanates daily from *Khorev*" (*Pirkei Avot* 6:2). It is worth noting that one of the meanings of the root of *Khorev* is "to destroy, to lay waste." The experience of the Divine Voice shatters the conventional view of life. It liberates us from our enslavement to the myriad illusions and idols to which we are prey. But we are always left with the challenge of retaining and recalling those visions so that we can live in accordance with them.

One of the major functions of religion is to facilitate the retaining and recalling of these moments of illumination and to catalyze this quality of consciousness. Among the components comprising organized religion, it is only the more radical aspects, if any, that overlap with mystical spirituality. The more mainstream acceptance attained by a religion, the more marginalized mystical elements tend to become. Since one's spiritual allegiance must ultimately be towards God rather than towards the tradition, the tradition must function as a means towards spiritual cultivation, for which it can provide a framework when it maintains a balance between structure and the freedom that growth requires. A combination of democratic religious sensibilities and a focus on Divine "Being" rather that Divine "doing" can help keep the cultivation of consciousness primary.

An expansion or leap of consciousness is a form of revelation. Revelation is the peak of all perceptions. However, revelation can be understood in various ways. An understanding that focuses on a supernatural or "miraculous" revelation doesn't transform a person in the way that an illumination of consciousness can. The level of awareness that perceives "being" as miraculous is a much more sublime spiritual state than a belief in supernatural miracles or a belief of any sort. Revelation that is an expansion of consciousness, a deepened awareness of the Omnipresent One, can occur at any moment. All such revelations imply an exodus from our previous state. An exodus that does not include a transformed consciousness allows the idols and illusions of our past to accompany us to wherever we may journey. One of the idols and illusions of our past is the attachment to an anthropomorphic deity, no matter how subtly understood or depicted. The belief in supernatural miracles is often an important component of this form of idolatry.

Idolatry exists on many levels, however. Whenever we confound our means with our ends we render those means into a form of idolatry. The rigidity that often permeates the tradition can turn it into *avodah zarah*, idolatry, itself. There is a dialectical relationship between our view of who and what *adam* is or what Torah truly means and our experience and understanding of God. Torah as illuminated teaching is an open-ended quest towards an ever-increasing awareness of Divinity, rather than a sealed document with very fixed boundaries. The Torah, the sealed document, is a rich and vital arena for this quest, but not the only such arena. Ultimately Torah both emanates from an encounter with the living Divine Presence and catalyzes encounters of this nature. Nothing rivals an experience of God's Presence, which can often startle us into recognizing that we inadvertently have been idolatrous too. Understanding ourselves as embodied spiritual beings can help us focus on practical paths towards living in accordance with our insights and deepening them when God's immediacy recedes from our vision.

Kavana and meditative prayer are two interrelated powerful keys to cultivating our spiritual senses. Both are lifelong practices whose fruits are generally born out over time, but without any guarantees. *Kavana*, the focusing of our consciousness, can apply to every lived moment and help us engage it more deeply. In the arena of prayer it facilitates our entering and becoming the very words we pray, "living" them, rather than merely reciting them. Of course, each act or word is its own reward and our choice of words in prayer facilitates or inhibits our ability to enter them. However potent they may be, words remain tools. The careful choice of words and the *kavana* of attempting to enter them in prayer can take us to the point beyond which the silence of meditation becomes the appropriate *niggun* or music.

All of our acts are an expression and outgrowth of our state of being and consciousness. Meditation is the exercise and cultivation of consciousness. Though there are many different methods of meditation, the type I have focused on in this book is that which attempts to attain an awareness of *Ayin*, of the eternal in the ephemeral, the infinite Oneness that permeates and transcends all of existence. Meditation, of course, needs to exist in the context of a life of moral behavior and acts of love, kindness, and compassion. Each component feeds the others. Jewish meditation, as an attempt to cultivate our awareness of the Divine Presence, can revitalize our lives and our Jewish practices. It may make God a living Presence in our lives, rather than a mere belief. At the same time, an immediate experience of Divinity can lead one to draw into question those aspects of the tradition that inhibit our awareness of God rather than enhance it.

Sacred Myths Serve Consciousness, Not Replace It

Even the greatest myths are there to serve consciousness, not to replace it. We inherit the myths of our culture. They are ours if we embrace them. They are not here to enslave us and keep us out of the Promised Land, but to guide us and lead us towards it. Just as the meaning of a word or a ritual evolves with time, the meaning, role, and significance of a myth also evolves.

How do the major focal points of spiritual/national life play themselves out in the Torah? First, consciousness of the One God blossoms in the homeland among the patriarchs and matriarchs. Then the people go into exile in *Mitzrayim* (Egypt, metaphorically the "narrow places") and become enslaved there. Then they are taken out by Moses and brought to the wilderness of Sinai, where they experience revelation, followed by the journey back to the Promised Land to live a holy life faithful to the Divine revelation. Though Moses is the greatest of all teachers, he cannot accompany the nation there; we still have to enter the Promised Land without him. This story is applicable to the journey that every individual and every generation must make.

The Promised Land, in a psychological and spiritual sense, might be better understood as an orienting point rather than a final destination. Life is always evolving, and our perspective on where we are headed has to change as our vantage points shift toward the approaching horizon that orients us. Moses could give us the benefit of his great vision and provide tools to help us, but he could not build the Promised Land.

The generation that had been slaves in *Mitzrayim* could not enter the land and build the new society. In our own day, what Judaism and Jewishness will evolve into can only be realized by the generations after those traumatized by the Holocaust. The survivors are our parents (or grandparents). We love and honor them. No one should be criticized for not shattering the yoke that broke their back. Nor could we expect them not to be focused on the primary Jewish experience of their lives.

We repeat the story of the enslavement in *Mitzrayim* and the exodus through the generations by retelling it, learning from it, and reliving its psychological/spiritual essentials throughout our lives. But our main task is to build the New Land. Jewish tradition has created many moving rituals around the stories of enslavement, exodus, and revelation, but not around entering the Promised Land and building a holy and just life there, that is, living as fully as possible according to our visions *beyn adam lamakom* (between humans and the Omnipresent) and *beyn adam lakhavero* (between humans).

"Mitpardesim"—Those Who Seek "Pardes"

If we look at Judaism historically, we cannot ignore its evolution. Though the *m'kubalim*, the Kabbalists, saw themselves as carrying on the traditions of the patriarchs and earlier mystics such as the *yordei merkavah*, "the descenders to the Divine Chariot," they themselves had created a different "school." Though the Hasidim drew much from previous mystical paths, they by and large were not orthodox Kabbalists. Similarly, those who find great spiritual sustenance and inspiration in the mystical schools of the past, but cannot in good faith be orthodox adherents of them for various reasons *"l'shem shamayim"* (for the sake of heaven), might well be called *"mitpardesim,"* those who seek *pardes*.

In the biblical story of the twelve scouts who went to spy out the Promised Land, only two could see their future in it. The other ten were frightened. They were typical of their generation, who said, "Were there not enough graves in *Mitzrayim* that you brought us into the wilderness to die?" (Exodus 14:11)—in other words, it would be better to go back to *Mitzrayim* that to die in the wilderness.

And who were the two who saw the future in the Promised Land? *Calev* (Caleb) and *Yehoshua* (Joshua). *"Calev"* means "like the heart" and *Yehoshua* means *"Yah* [God] is my salvation." At times our ancestors, like ourselves, have been too afraid to enter the Promised Land, despite the best intentions. Yet entering and building the Promised Land is a perennial aspiration. We have clung to the familiar, making idols of the temporary "truths" of the past. We must empower ourselves and our descendents with all that we have received from our ancestors, struggled with, and learned. We must encourage the coming generations to transcend our limitations, though it may be painful to see our own life's work left behind when it once was the horizon looming before us. In this way we will always be involved in the building and the promise of the Promised Land.